Internet for Active Learners:

Curriculum-Based Strategies for K·12

Pam
Berger

DISCARD

AMERICAN LIBRARY ASSOCIATION
Chicago and London
1998

Trademarked names appear in the text of this book. Rather than identify or insert a trademark symbol at the appearance of each name, the authors and the American Library Association state that the names are used for editorial purposes exclusively, to the ultimate benefit of the owners of the trademarks. There is absolutely no intention of infringement on the rights of the trademark owners.

"Student of the Future," illustration on cover and page 1, by Dean Yeagle

The paper used in this publication meets the minimum requirements of American National Standard for Information Sciences—Permanence of Paper for Printed Library Materials, ANSI Z39.48-1992. ∞

Library of Congress Cataloging-in-Publication Data
Berger, Pam.
    Internet for active learners: curriculum-based strategies for
  K.12/Pam Berger.
      p.   cm.
    Includes bibliographical references and index.
    ISBN 0-8389-3487-0
    1. Computer network resources—Study and teaching (Elementary)—
  United States. 2. Computer network resources—Study and teaching
  (Secondary)—United States. 3. Active learning—United States.
  4. School libraries—Activity programs—United States.   I. Title.
  ZA4201.B47   1998
  025.04'071—dc21   98-23102

Printed in the United States of America.

02 01 00 99   5 4 3 2

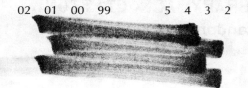

Contents

Foreword

Many have tried to explain what the Internet is and what its component pieces can do for information seekers. Explanations exist in a variety of printed guides and on the Web itself. Workshops, training sessions, and courses on Internet access are now offered in every educational delivery mode—from written text to electronically accessed course. No one has described the Web as an organized, easily accessed place. Most experts agree that jumping in without a game plan is like navigating in a bottomless pit.

At the same time, the American public is asking questions about how students are being prepared to work in this increasingly electronic world, a world that is becoming more and more dependent on information and ideas shared via the Internet's World Wide Web. Teachers and school library media specialists are in the business of meeting this challenge. Both are committed to helping students learn to solve problems by learning how to ask the right questions, finding appropriate information sources, and evaluating them. Teachers and school library media specialists realize that learning how to access the World Wide Web effectively has become a central curriculum concern. They have collaborated in the development of a special kind of student literacy: information literacy.

There was a time when teachers and professional information specialists in schools understood the structure and organization of available resources in many formats. They could identify and suggest the best match between what existed in a subject area and a learner's need for information. Their information world was a comfortable, describable place. But that time has passed. No one is in control of everything that is available. The Internet is the premier example of the revolutionary change in resource access and the accompanying need for educators to reconceptualize what access to information and ideas involves and how this new access model can be incorporated into active curriculum.

The bottomless pit of the World Wide Web demands the development of new mental models for professionals and their students. Cognitive psychologists tell us that individuals have internalized models of the processes they follow. They develop these models through practice and through observation of others. Often the information search process fails because the searcher has an inadequate mental model to follow. The successful information navigator works with two distinct model dimensions: a revised understanding of the search process in a Web-based environment, and an expanded view of the resource world and how it is organized. The job of the educator is to ensure that students have the opportunities to create such intellectual models.

The American Association of School Librarians (AASL) has always been concerned with student literacy. This concern is reflected in the mission statement of the organization, its guidelines for practice, its programs, and its publications. Currently, two major efforts of the organization are moving the development of information literacy to the cutting edge. The first and more comprehensive effort is reflected in the publication of new national guidelines for educational practice. In 1998, AASL, in conjunction with AECT (the Association for Educational Communication and Technology), will publish guidelines that focus on information literacy and the role educators must play in enabling students to achieve it. *Internet for Active Learners: Curriculum-Based Strategies for K.12* is a superb guide to practical applications.

The second major association effort is also supported by the intellectual focus of this book: using AASL's ICONnect initiative to assist learners to become actively engaged in their own learning by connecting them and their teachers to relevant curriculum-related sites on the World Wide Web.

The beauty of ICONnect is in its utility to help the field meet the challenges of the guidelines. Its On-Line Courses provide directions in using the Internet to make curriculum connections. Its Curriculum Connections component is structured to provide advice on exemplary Internet sites and to answer technology questions. Through its Minigrants, curriculum-based collaborative projects of school library media specialists and teachers are rewarded and further education is encouraged. And the training provided by its KidsConnect question-and-answer service is building a cadre of expert professional Internet users in schools.

I met Pam Berger many years ago when she was responsible for Databases in Schools, a unique set of program meetings that extended school library media practice to the online world. Her 1994 handbook and directory, *CD-ROM for Schools,* was a welcome addition to the collection development literature. She continues to expand what we know about locating and using electronic resources in her newsletter, *Information Searcher.* And now she brings her foresight and practical experience to *Internet for Active Learners: Curriculum-Based Strategies for K.12,* a guidebook to information technology applications in the curriculum of the school. Pam Berger's leadership has inspired the ICONnect initiative and its entire wonderful offspring, of which this book is just one.

Jacqueline C. Mancall
Professor of Information Studies
Drexel University
College of Information Science
and Technology
Philadelphia

Preface

It's hard to open an education magazine these days without seeing an article about computers revolutionizing schools. Some praise computers for their ability to deliver effective instruction, customized to an individual's learning style. Others decry technology, citing evidence that students can't possibly learn off the screen. Some fear that the rise of the computer comes at the expense of humanism, that we are raising a nation of automatons unable to relate to each other. General magazines like *Atlantic Monthly* and others have brought the debate to a more general forum. Politicians pledge to wire every school and every library to the Internet. And once you're wired, you can go to the Web and find the debate raging there. While we stake out our positions, we all know that truth lies somewhere between the extremes. As educators, we've seen the difference an excellent teacher can make, as well as the failures of the mediocre. We've seen software that truly engages students in active learning and programs that merely digitize learning by rote.

I have had the privilege of working for the past 13 years at Byram Hills High School in Armonk, New York, with administrators and faculty that supported me in my journey to understand and use technology for student learning. When I put an IBM PC XT in my library in 1984, I learned early on that the gift of educational technology was also a responsibility. With the funding came expectations. My school is in no way typical of others across the nation. However, whether your school library hosts a stand-alone machine or a school-wide fiber-optic network, and whenever your system was installed, the end results need to be the same—student learning.

I often remind myself that my role in educating students is to prepare them to be information literate for the twenty-first century. Technology is a means, not an end. How can I use these tools to engage students in active learning, to integrate information resources into the curriculum, to teach information literacy within the context of the curriculum? These are the questions I address in *Internet for Active Learners: Curriculum-Based Strategies for K.12.*

Many schools are funding technology without thoughtful planning. No instructions included. Buying a top-of-the-line set of tools does not make you a carpenter. I feel strongly that our professional associations should lead the way in effective use of technology. During a reception at the 1994 conference of the American Association of School Librarians in Indianapolis, surrounded by high-tech exhibits at the Indianapolis Children's Museum, Mike Eisenberg, Jackie Mancall, and I talked about this need. Our conversation was the beginning of AASL's ICONnect initiative, which I have chaired. A team of energetic and passionate volunteers has led the way in developing online resources for the profession. By 1998, more than 5,000 thousand educators have taken our online classes. Our KidsConnect virtual reference service, supported by a team of more than 200 school librarians, has answered more than 10,000 questions from students. Our curriculum connections team selected the best Web sites for educating students. Fourteen ICONnect Minigrants have been awarded to teams of school library media specialists and teachers for developing exemplary Internet-integrated curriculum units. The ICONnect Home Page has consistently been among the 12 most frequently hit pages of the ALA site from a possibility of approximately 1,100 pages.

While the ICONnect team anticipated and planned for a bounty of digital resources, we did not forget print. AASL launched the ICONnect Publication Series with two introductory booklets, *How to Connect to the Internet,* soon followed by *Curriculum Connection on the Net.* With *Internet for Active Learners,* I am addressing educators and librarians of various levels of expertise. For the newbies, I have described in plain language the basics of what the Internet is in chapter 2. Advanced users will want to skip chapter 2 and skim through chapter 3, where I run through common Internet applications. The rest of the book is for newbies and netheads alike because it is about learning and teaching. Throughout the chapters I have highlighted tips to keep in mind, and for adept Internet users looking for new challenges, I recommend advance strategies.

Naturally, from the very conception of this book, I faced the challenge of writing about a subject as fluid as the Internet. Fortunately, while I reveal the bedrock of active learning on the Internet in these static, high-resolution, linear pages, I can accommodate the fluid nature of the Web with pointers to two sites. Go to your computer now and bookmark these two sites. I will reference them throughout the book.

 ICONnect. The American Association of School Librarians' technology initiative connects learners to information using the Internet. ICONnect is a strategy for school librarians and other educators to acquire the skills necessary to be information literate in the twenty-first century. Free online courses, lists of evaluated, annotated Web sites for K–12, Q&A service for kids, mini-grants, and listservs are interrelated to create a professional community of learners targeted to understanding and using the Internet in K–12 education. Visit the ICONnect Web site at http://www.ala.org/ICONN to learn more.

 CyberTours. Pam Berger's Information Searcher, a newsletter for using CD-ROMs and the Internet in education, and Tramline Inc., the online education company, have joined forces to produce an electronic extension of this book. Each CyberTour, designed by the author, uses unique online software, developed by Tramline Inc. (http://www.tramline.com) that works on both Macintosh and Windows platforms. It automatically guides the user through preselected Web sites to explore a curriculum-based theme or teaching strategy, expanding the content, concepts, and theory outlined in this book. The CyberTour site is free and available to all educators who want to learn how to use the Internet to create active learning environments in their libraries and classrooms. Logon the CyberTours Home Page and enjoy the ride at http://www.infosearcher.com/cybertours

One of the rewards of working with ICONnect has been collaborating with so many dedicated, knowledgeable librarians and other professionals. I owe a special thanks to the entire ICONnect Team without whom ICONnect would only have been an engaging conversation. I especially want to thank Jackie Mancall, who as AASL President worked hard to create ICONnect and continues as a driving force behind it, and Mike Eisenberg for his vision of KidsConnect and continuous support. Thanks go to Sandi Block, Susan Kinnell Carty, Jackie Cohen, Phyllis Di Bianco, Carol Kroll, Barbara Stripling, Lisa Wolfe, and Rennie Wrubel, whose guidance and friendship are invaluable. Others deserve thanks also: GraceAnne DeCandido who helped tighten up the manuscript, and my editor, Patrick Hogan, who steadfastly believed this book would get published and prodded me on with humor and skillful editorial guidance. And to my strongest supporters, Bill, Kathryn, and Chris—a big hug!

Pam Berger

The ICONnect Way: Becoming a Twenty-first Century Librarian

Navigator: Learn How to Navigate and Effectively Search the Internet

- Are you new to the Internet? Sign up for the online course, IBASICS, to jumpstart your learning.

- Learn tips and strategies to effectively search the Web. Sign up for these online courses: Navigating the Web, Using Search Engines Effectively, and Advanced Search Engines.

- Do you sometimes get frustrated when using the Internet? Join the TECHDISC listserv to network with colleagues and get your questions answered about navigating and searching the Internet.

Teacher/Facilitator: Integrate Information Literacy Skills into the Curriculum Using the Internet

- Teach students to be information literate in a technological world. Sign up for the online course, Information Literacy and the Internet.

- Learn how to integrate Internet resources into the curriculum. Sign up for these online courses: Integrating Internet into the Curriculum, Internet and the Elementary Curriculum, and Telecollaborative Activities on the Internet.

- Reach out to your faculty and teach them how to integrate Internet resources into the curriculum. Logon to the Curriculum Connection section of the ICONnect Web site for evaluated, annotated Web sites for K–12 education. Download and distribute them to teachers with a personal note from you.

- Check out the KidsConnect Q & A Service and the KidsConnect Favorite Web sites for the best Web sites to answer kids' questions. Send your faculty an e-mail with the KidsConnect Web site URL.

- Collaboratively develop curriculum integrating Internet resources. Team with a teacher to apply for an ICONnect Minigrant and win $1,000.

- Discuss relevant issues, theories, and strategies to integrate Internet resources into the curriculum. Join ICONCUR listserv to join your colleagues and contribute to the discussion.

Evaluator: Evaluate and Organize Information for Students and Teachers

- Logon to the Curriculum Connections section of the ICONnect Web site and download the Web Evaluation Form. Cut and paste the form, modifying it for your use as you teach students and faculty to evaluate Web sites.
- Sign up for the online course, Evaluating Web Sites.
- Join ICONCUR listserv to discuss Web evaluation and its role in curriculum/technology integration.

Publisher: Organize and Contribute to the Knowledge on the Web

- Learn how to develop a library home page to guide and instruct students and faculty in using Web resources. Sign up for an online course, Developing Content for Library Home Pages.
- When developing your library Web site, check out Curriculum Connections' annotated Web sites and KidsConnect's favorite Web sites.
- Join the TECHDISC listserv to find answers to your technical questions while developing your library Web site.

Information Manager: Take a Leadership Role in the Development, Design, and Policies for Information Access

- Understand the issues surrounding electronic information access. Sign up for the online course, Internet Issues K–12 to learn about Acceptable Use Policies, filters, and more.
- Logon to the Curriculum Connections section of the ICONnect Web Site for updated reports and documents such as the ALA Bill of Rights, ALA Resolutions on filtering software, sample AUPs, and more.
- Join the TECHDISC listserv and join in the discussion about hardware and software issues that affect information access.

Staff Developer: Take a Lead Role in Teaching Faculty and Parents to Understand and Use the Internet Effectively

- Learn how to assume the leadership role in your building. Sign up for the online course, The School Library Media Specialist of the 21st Century.
- Reach out to parents and teach them how to effectively use the Internet with their kids.
- Sign up for the online course, Learning Partners: Parents and Children Together on the Internet, to get a complete PowerPoint presentation, a list of good Web sites for parents, and more.
- Sponsor a Technology Night for parents and demonstrate the ICONnect FamiliesConnect home page, designed specifically for parents, grandparents, aunts, uncles, etc., to learn about the Internet.
- Look at some "best practices" incorporating Internet into the curriculum when working with teachers. Logon to the ICONnect Web site and look at the Minigrants award winners.

Lifelong Learner: Keep an Open Mind to New Technologies and New Ways of Teaching and Learning

- Learn about new technologies. Sign up for the online course, New Trends in Interactivity on the Internet.
- Keep your electronic reference skills fine-tuned. Get trained online to become a KidsConnect volunteer.
- Keep abreast of important issues. Sign up for the online course, Internet Issues K–12, to learn about copyright, filters, AUPs, and more.
- Join your colleagues on the ICONCURR listserv to discuss the important issues surrounding curriculum/technology integration.
- Join AASL and take a leadership role in teaching and learning in the 21st century.

CyberTours

CyberTour: Transformational Technologies

What new technologies will have an impact on teaching and learning in the future? Hop on the CyberTour bus to learn about new Internet technologies being developed for the Web: streaming audio and video, MOOs, VRML, video conferencing, and more. (See the Preface for Information Searcher's CyberTours Web site address.)

CyberTour: Active Learning Sites

Why the Internet? Find out why the Internet is such a powerful educational tool. Take a virtual tour of the Web to visit sites where students collaborate, locate primary resources, publish their work, and experience the Web as an active learning environment.

CyberTour: Search Strategies

How do I find information on the Internet? Join a CyberTour to learn some strategies and tips to effectively use search engines and subject directories to satisfy your information needs—quickly and efficiently.

CyberTour: Web Evaluation Guide

How do you evaluate Web sites? Hop onboard a CyberTour to learn how to identify good Web sites for K–12 by visiting some good and some not-so-good sites. Learn some tips and strategies to teach students this valuable twenty-first century skill.

CyberTour: Weaving a Web-Based Curriculum

How do you integrate the Internet into your curriculum? Take a CyberTour and learn some strategies that incorporate Internet resources and use the unique features of the Internet to motivate, involve, and challenge students to become active learners.

CyberTour: Reference on the Web

Take a tour through the Web to view unique Web resources that support and enhance curriculum. Look at the valuable primary resources, value-added curriculum collections, in-depth reference sites, and more.

CyberTour: Building Your Library Web Site

Why does every school library need a home page? Join a CyberTour and learn how school librarians are using home pages as instructional, communication, and public relations tools. Visit some of the best school library sites and learn how to develop a home page for your library.

CyberTour: Teaching the Internet

How do you teach about the Internet using the Internet? Learn about Web sites that will help students, teachers, and parents to navigate and use the Web. Take a CyberTour to visit exemplary Web sites that teach about the features and functions of the Web.

Chapter 1

Future Students, Future Librarians

Yo, Socrates!

Let me introduce myself. No, I'm not the ancient philosophy-type guy, although we are alike in some ways since we share a similar approach to learning. I'm the student of the future. You would remember my parents—they were in school in the late 1990s. They would stop in the library media center, search the online catalogs and a few CD-ROMs; they even had access to the first generation of the Web. But it's different for me—I don't go into the library. But wait. Don't get me wrong here. It's not that I don't use the library, it's just that it's not a location. Library is more of a process now. It's the focus of everything I do. Learning is active and collaborative, and you're nowhere if you're not top-notch info-literate.

I know what you are thinking. "What is that thing Socrates is wearing? A PC? A telephone? A television? A cybernetic research assistant? A book?" Well, it's all of the above. When it's a telephone, it gives you real-time language translation. At least most languages—I still can't quite get Swahili yet, but, still, I can talk with tons of other students and teachers all around the planet. And if I pop up my trusty handheld digital camera, I get high-definition pictures, plus all the regular information. The twenty-first century technologies—television, telephone and computers—all combined and ZAP! We get telecomputers that are interactive and intelligent. It's my own personal research assistant—one with intelligent knowledge navigation who finds information through instantaneous wireless communications in comprehensive databases.

I also have a handheld computer. The audio manual lets you know that it combines the portability of a handheld business calculator with the power of a desktop PC, all for only ten ounces. And look, no keyboard! I use my light pen for pointing or crossing out and such, and voice synthesizing for everything else. It knows my voice and follows my instructions.

My "textbooks" are in my vest pockets. Schools set up a good system. Each school district has a central production unit in which the CD discs can be mastered and personalized to each class. The teachers choose the chapters, which can be placed in any order, and information for the Web can easily be downloaded and integrated. The system is interactive. Students can add data through voice technology or mark certain passages or sections of the text with pen point technology. In this way note taking is integrated to the content. Notes are shared through groupware programs. Hot buttons offer fast and easy access to information on the disc and the relevant sites on the Internet. The computer screen resolution is good, and we rarely need to print out text.

Information is easily transferable to small palm tops or to family home communications center.

Access to wireless telecommunications is universal, from outside the school building and through the school network. We communicate with our classmates in online learning communities, receive e-mail messages from friends, and edit reports and notes from teachers. The school library is accessed in the same way: stock market reports for economics class, up-to-the-minute news for social studies discussion classes, the latest scientific research, and of course, e-mail from my school librarian. She is helping me develop strategies to locate and evaluate the information I need. Everyone is networked through radio signals; no more plugging into phone jacks! Computers are set on a host-ready mode.

I even get messages from my Mom. "Socrates, don't forget your dentist appointment after soccer practice. . . ."

Yo, enough said. You get the idea—the school library is a *process*, the most important one, and always available. The walls came tumbling down and the library media center is now everywhere, guiding me through the information maze. Later. See you in the future—we'll rap on the Net.

ADVANCED STRATEGY
Logon to PointCast Technologies at http://www.pointcast.com to experience Push Media. This site allows the users to pick and choose the type of information to be delivered, seamlessly and effortlessly, through an information channel to their computer. Pointcast will customize the up-to-the-minute news and information and deliver it to your computer. ·

SOCRATES' LEARNING ENVIRONMENT

Socrates' world is a seamless electronic environment without walls; it is transparent, a "virtual reality." It is composed of a global network or matrix of digital data—anything that can be digitized such as text, graphics, interviews, photos, sounds, animation, numbers, maps, etc. It's independent from time and place constraints, sending information to wherever Socrates is at the moment for "just in time" delivery. School libraries concentrate on information access rather than acquisition, giving Socrates unlimited resources relevant to his information and curriculum needs.[1]

ADVANCED STRATEGY
Experience life in a virtual world. Logon to Worlds Inc. at http://www.worlds.net to learn how virtual worlds are being used. Download software so you can enter and explore Worlds Chat and Alpha World, three-dimensional multi-user environments, and find out how educators can get a free three-dimensional toolkit to create virtual worlds with students.

Socrates' world emphasizes student-centered, constructionist, resource-based learning and project-oriented, authentic assessment. But at the heart of it is information literacy that is synonymous with knowing how to learn. The ability to access, evaluate, and use information effectively is a basic survival skill of the twenty-first century. He has learned how to forage for data, filtering, synthesizing, and organizing incoming information to reveal patterns and relationships. Traditional forms of learning have evolved into deeply personal, information-immersion experiences. Interacting with information is central to Socrates' learning and his participation in the twenty-first century society.

ADVANCED STRATEGY

Take a look at the visual computer software tools available to help students to organize, solve problems, and think analytically. Logon on to http://www.inspiration.com and http://www.mindman.com. Download demonstration copies of the software programs and test them out with your students. For more information on using visual tools in education, read David Hyerle's book, *Visual Tools,* published by the Association for Supervision and Curriculum Development in Alexandria.

Virtual communities have been developed to structure the learning experience in cyberspace. Demands of the future and the increasing capabilities of emerging information technology produced new forms of communication and interactive, collaborative learning. Now, in the year 2015, Socrates participates in "Knowledge Webs" that include online archival resources and virtual exhibits that duplicate real-world settings, somewhat like museums. Distributed curriculum projects, especially in science and mathematics, allow for sharing experiments across time and place. His teachers guide Socrates to move beyond assimilating facts and into generating mental models. Teacher-created learning experiences structure and highlight new ideas, providing insight and knowledge.

TIP

Visit a virtual school electronically. Logon on to Web66's list of "online" schools on the Web at http://web66.coled.umn.edu/schools/Lists/Online.html.

Using "groupware" tools, Socrates collaborates with classmates, experts, and teachers. He regularly joins distributed conferences that provide an instant network of contacts with useful skills and "just in time answers" to immediate questions. Formal education comprises only a small fraction of how he spends his time; he still has face-to-face interactions, but these are not in the mid-twentieth century model of a classroom full of passive learners in rows of desks.

Shared synthetic environments and simulations extend Socrates' experiences past what he can encounter in the real world. He enters and explores the simulations, gathers information, analyzes, makes decisions, and reacts to his artificial environment. It's a total learning environment, a place to be, not just a communications channel. Artificial intelligence, expert systems, hypertext, and knowbots that navigate cyberspace are part of his research toolbox. Computer programs and utilities offer customized information, creating links with pertinent information to create meaningful connections for learning.

TRANSFORMATIONAL TECHNOLOGIES
What new technologies will have an impact on teaching and learning in the future? Hop on the CyberTour bus to learn about new Internet technologies being developed for the Web—streaming audio and video, MOOs, VRML, video conferencing, and more. (See the Preface for Information Searcher's CyberTours Web site address.)

SOCRATES' COMPETENCIES

Socrates is information literate; he is an expert at accessing, evaluating, and using information, a necessity for project-based learning. Knowing that accurate and comprehensive information is the basis for intelligent decision making, he emphasizes accessing information efficiently and effectively. He recognizes that, when he needs information, his first task is to develop a few thoughtful questions that highlight or target the main concepts. This helps him understand the information problem so he can identify a variety of potential information sources and develop a strategy for locating the information. Sometimes he needs to be recursive, re-evaluating his course with the introduction of new data. Creativity usually comes into play as well, when he notices chance findings and follows his intuitive insights.

TIP
To examine Socrates' information literacy competencies in depth, look at AASL/AECT Information Literacy Standards at http://www.ala.org/AASL/stndsdrft5.html.

As he gathers information, Socrates constantly determines its accuracy, relevance, and comprehensiveness, distinguishing among fact, point of view, and opinion to select information appropriate to the problem or question he is researching. Socrates continues organizing the information; screening, sorting and analyzing the data; building and testing mental models; and comparing it all to what he already knows about the subject. The process requires him to integrate knowledge, analyze relationships, and incorporate personal experiences. Depending on the learning experience, he will demonstrate what he has learned by solving a problem, constructing a model, or defending a supportable position.

All of this is done collaboratively within his electronic learning community and with his teacher and library media specialist coaching and facilitating his learning. They have structured the environment to ensure learning occurs, actively guiding Socrates and assessing his learning as he progresses.

As you can clearly see, in the year 2015 there has been a shift in education, and especially in how kids learn. Classroom lectures have been replaced by computer networked access to educational resources. Students are no longer passive recipients but rather self-directed learners. The emphasis switched from individual learning to team learning, collaborating in multiple electronic environments. The twentieth century stable educational content was replaced by rapidly changing content presented in a wide range of formats. Schools no longer just deliver instructional services but require that all students learn at a high level. A teacher's job is no longer to cover the curriculum but to enable diverse learners to construct their own knowledge. Technologies that encourage, support, and extend collaboration, that use learning by doing and knowledge acquisition, are the key underpinnings in Socrates' world.

Libraries of the future have also shifted. We can postulate two visions. If we are indeed entering an age when meaningful organization of information will be a paramount asset in the world, then the library as the institution responsible for organizing, presenting, and codifying knowledge will be responsible for leading the charge. If we are indeed entering an age of educational reform that demands students to think critically and be able to judge the validity of massive amounts of information available to them, then the school library will be a leader in this reform.

TIP

To learn more about the power of telecomputing, visit the Global Schoolhouse Web site, http://www.gsn.org/index.html, choose the Our Articles section, and read *Global Literacy in a Gutenberg Culture* and *Collaboration in the Classroom and over the Internet.*

On the other hand, if we view the concept of a library more narrowly, as a room containing neatly organized stacks of books with librarians who lend out these objects to students, then our long-term prognosis is dismal. Raymond Kurzweil, a noted author, inventor, and authority on artificial intelligence, uses an amusing metaphor to describe the situation. If you were a blacksmith at the turn of the century, your outlook would depend on whether you saw yourself as a shaper of horse shoes or a facilitator of transportation—in which case you would turn in your forge and hammer for a gas pump. With the pace of change accelerating, it is not only the private sector that must change dramatically. Technological change affects most institutions, including schools and libraries, so that we must define our mission broadly enough to survive obsolescence of more narrowly defined self-concepts and be ready to meet Socrates' information needs.

School Librarian as Cybrarian

Tim Berners-Lee, the inventor of the World Wide Web, when asked why he developed the WWW, replied that he did it for three reasons. The first was to give people up-to-date information at their fingertips by giving them personal power to hypertext. The second goal was the realization of an information space where everyone could share and contribute their ideas and solutions. The third was the creation of agents to integrate the information with real life so enormous amounts of information would no longer be lost. Some of his vision has come to fruition—we do hypertext to enormous amounts of information with just a point-and-click and we do have access to information that was lost or out of reach to many of us before the Web. But these processes are in their infancy, especially in the education world. Schools are just getting involved and learning how to use this new information tool both for information retrieval and for sharing ideas and solutions. School librarians have the opportunity to be a key player in the development and use of the Internet in their school as they redefine their roles in a global network environment to emerge as Cybrarians.

Cybrarians are Internet navigators, teachers, and facilitators; publishers, staff developers, information evaluators, planners, and policy makers; and lifelong learners. Whether you have a full network of computers with Internet access or just one stand-alone computer with modem access to the Internet, your library is affected by the introduction of the Internet. Take some time to consider how the Internet will expand your role—from librarian to cybrarian.

School Librarian as Internet Navigator

Navigating information is one of the traditional jobs that librarians are familiar with and one that easily carries forward to the electronic library world. Increasingly, librarians help students and teachers navigate purposefully through oceans of data to locate information to answer "essential questions." They guide learners through a wealth of information resources, helping them decide if a book, a CD-ROM resource, a video, a magazine article, an online database, or a Web site is the best place to locate the information they need. School librarians help them develop strategies to find the best and fastest route to databases, reports, articles, statistics, reviews, graphics, software, news, and other information items. They help students, teachers, and parents make the connection between information and learning, helping them become successful Internet navigators themselves.

School Librarian as Teacher and Facilitator

School librarians are facilitators or guides. They help students develop strategies to locate and access information and teach them how to develop information literacy skills. They help students understand the organization of information from one discipline to another and from one format to another. They teach how to use search engines and directories effectively and how to use, save, and organize bookmarks for easy retrieval at a later time. They show how to download, decompress, and open documents and programs from the Internet, as well as how to record electronic sources of information and to properly cite and give credit to authors. School librarians collaborate with teachers to integrate these skills into the context of the curriculum along with curriculum objectives and information skills.

School Librarian as Publisher

School librarians add content and editorial value to the Internet in designing and writing home pages. Just as previously they developed pathfinders, bibliographies, brochures, and flyers, they now organize electronic information. Resource guides on library home pages assist students, teachers, administrators, and parents to use the Internet in a meaningful and purposeful way. Web sites in the resource guide, which have been identified because of their relevance to the school curriculum, are evaluated and annotated for efficient access. In addition, school librarians develop guides for using search engines effectively and tools for evaluating the Internet. When sharing on the Internet, librarians offer education and non-education users valuable guidance.

School Librarian as Information Evaluator

Thanks to new information technologies, we can access more information in less time, but the challenge of developing insight from all this information may be compounded by an overabundance of data. Alvin Toffler warned of "info-glut" while Peter Drucker claims that information overload leads to "information blackout." Finding information is not the problem, but separating relevant, accurate information from the information deluge is difficult. School librarians help students and teachers evaluate Web sites for accuracy, authority, and content. They develop evaluation tools and actively integrate evaluation skills into the context of the curriculum. They assist students as they assess and judge quality, developing life-long information literacy strategies.

School Librarian as Information Manager

The question is not as simple as connecting classrooms and information systems. Important questions need to be addressed, and the school librarian as the information manager needs to address them. What information will reside on the network? Which CD-ROM will circulate and why? Can a single CD-ROM encyclopedia service all 45 classrooms? Should it be multimedia or not? Should we purchase access to a Web encyclopedia? How many users can access the Internet at one time? Is this important to the student learning outcomes? Understandably, connectivity is not the goal. As a manager you need to help shape the written policies that enhance and strengthen access to data for everyone in the learning communities. School librarians along with other educators need to ask the question, "What's in it for students?" If the technology does not have an impact on the teaching and learning process, then we should not be expending the energy and money.

School Librarian as Staff Developer

School librarians have a unique opportunity to take a leadership role in introducing and teaching the Internet to faculty, administrators, and parents. School district staffs are becoming more and more involved in seeking and taking advantage of opportunities to improve their professional skills and increase their effectiveness in using technology. School librarians, with their knowledge and experience of information systems, the information search process, teaching, and curriculum are in a pivotal position to develop and offer staff development. As the library walls come down and information is accessed across school networks, teachers will need to know how to guide students in locating, evaluating, and using information. School librarians will teach teachers so they, in turn, can assist students.

School Librarian as Lifelong Learner

The school librarian's two professional arenas, the library/information world and the education world, are both in flux. Due to technology and innovations in information delivery, librarians are being challenged to learn new ways of doing business. School as we know it will change, and our role within the teaching and learning process will need to adapt to meet the changing needs of students and teachers. Lifelong learners will take on new dimensions, learning from other teachers within a mentoring environment, learning from students in a shared inquiry environment, and sometimes learning online in a virtual environment. New configurations of learning and teaching will evolve, and school librarians will be in the forefront of their development as lifelong learners.

NOTE

1. H. King, "Walls around the Electronic Library," *Electronic Library* 11 (1993): 165.

Chapter 2

The Internet for Newbies

The Internet is a global network of computers, a network of networks, that allows many millions of computer users to share and exchange information. Hundreds of thousands of computers linked to the Internet hold vast quantities and varieties of data that you can access from your PC whenever you want to, wherever you are. Think of it in terms of a technology you use and are very familiar with—the phone system. When you make a telephone call, the phone company automatically routes your call through the available lines to connect your call to its intended destination. You can talk to anyone who has a phone connected to the system. Now, instead of a phone, think of computers all over the world connected in such a way that users can call them up and access them. If your computer is connected to the Internet, you can connect to any other computer that is connected and access and share information. It doesn't matter what type of computer you are logged on, everything from PCs to Macs to supercomputers all communicate using the same set of rules called TCP/IP (Transmission Control Protocol/Internet Protocol).

The Internet is also a network of services and resources to share data and publications. It brings the world to the classroom. Students around the globe can collaborate on special school projects such as a science class working with researchers in the Arctic region. Kids can look at graphics of the Dead Sea scrolls on file in the Library of Congress or download weather satellite photos of their region. The Internet brings the world of information into the school library media center, allowing students to share their experience, opinions, and information. It provides a way to create resources and share them with millions of people around the world.

The Internet facilitates collaborative learning. Conversations and discussions take place through ongoing interaction among peers and experts in electronic learning communities. Together they question, research, analyze, and discuss concepts, issues, and content to create and shape knowledge. Location is not an issue, nor is the time of day; participants just need to have a common learning goal.

The Internet makes learning global. Time, space, and location disappear as people join together to make learning more dynamic, more interesting, and more compelling to students. A sense of global community comes into play as students work with peers around the world to solve environmental issues, discuss popular music, and debate current events issues.

The Internet creates environments for students to be active learner and learn by doing. Rather than passively listening to a lecture given by a teacher, students direct their own learning by pursuing their interests and taking responsibility for managing their own projects. Students are involved in the subject, and through this two-way process, invest more mental energy and develop a more comprehensive understanding of the subject.

TIP
Learn how the Clinton administration plans to maximize the bene-fits of educational technology at http://www.whitehouse.gov/edtech.html.

The Internet provides students with the opportunity to do authentic tasks—to be scientists or writers or whatever. Students participate in telecollaborative projects by locating, accessing, and analyzing data electronically while working along side of scientists, writers, anthropologists, or mathematicians. Students are actively involved and solve real problems—testing their newly developed skills, locating the latest research, testing hypotheses, and collaborating with peers around the country. (See Figure 2.1.)

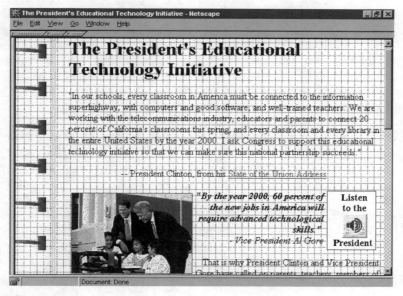

Figure 2.1
This Web site details government plans for using technology in education.

The Internet offers real-world examples of integrated knowledge. As students explore the Internet, they realize that information is organized in an interdisciplinary fashion, more reflective of real life than school. NASA keeps huge databases on mathematics as well as science topics. Economics sites reflect sociology and mathematics references.

TIP
The Teaching with Technology Web site (http://www.wam.umd.edu/
~mlhall/teaching.html) contains a varied and in-depth collection of
links that addresses using electronic technologies in the classroom.

The Internet is blind to one's cultural, gender, race, and physical abilities. A few years ago the *New Yorker* magazine printed a cartoon depicting two dogs talking. The dog who is sitting in front of a computer linked to the Internet says, "On the Internet, nobody knows you're a dog." Kids can't prejudge others by their skin color or physical disability or by what they are wearing or not wearing. Hearing-impaired kids may even have an advantage on the Internet because they are not distracted by outside noises. Students quickly learn that what they are being judged on is what they say and how they say it.

The Internet is the library. A study by Keith Curry Lance published in 1994 explored the impact of the availability of library resources on academic achievement. The study stated that student achievement is directly related to the availability of resource material and an active School Library Media Center.(http://www.ed.gov/databases/ERIC_Digests/ed372759.html). The Internet and all its rich resources is another tool in the school library media specialist's information tool bag along with books, CD-ROMs, videos, and audiotapes.

The Internet is the future. The Internet is not a fad; it's not going to go away, it's just going to get bigger. The Internet is changing how we do research, communicate, advertise, do business, and find information. Students need to learn basic technology skills, especially Internet navigation, to be able to take their place in society.

The Internet is a vital, exciting, motivating information source. Students can learn firsthand from eyewitness accounts from ordinary citizens in Russia during the break-up of the Soviet Union, South African children during the riots and final collapse of the apartheid system, or scientists at NASA discussing the Challenger disaster. When it comes to important news, the Internet is often the first place information is available—to the world.

ACTIVE LEARNING SITES
Why the Internet? Find out why the Internet is such a powerful educational tool. Take a virtual tour of the Web to visit sites where students collaborate, locate primary resources, publish their work, and experience the Web an active learning environment.

THE WORLD WIDE WEB

A major reason for the accelerated growth of the Internet in the past few years is the World Wide Web (also known as the Web or WWW). This simple but ingenious system allows users to interact with documents stored on remote computers across the Internet as if they were part of a single huge hypertext document. A hypertext document allows the user to navigate through it in a nonlinear/nonsequential manner by selecting parts of the text which are linked to other parts of the same document or documents. Hypermedia is a hypertext system that is not restricted to text documents but includes other media as well.

Although the Web was developed in 1992 by Tim Berners-Lee of CERN Laboratories, Geneva, the concept of hypertext has been around for a long time. Futurist Vannevar Bush first presented the concept in the July 1945 issue of the *Atlantic Monthly* in "We May Think" (http://www.isg.sfu.ca/~duchier/misc/vbush). In the 1960s, Ted Nelson lead the charge into hypertextual exploration using computers. He coined the actual term "hypertext" to describe a new type of document, a new literary genre of branching, non-sequential writings on the computer screen.

The Web is one of the most powerful educational tools on the Internet. Electronic communications and computers are changing the way we communicate, find information, do business, and teach. The Web is acting as a catalyst, both speeding this process up and shaping it at the same time. Since its popularization in 1993, it has caught on like wildfire, spreading through universities, government agencies, research facilities, businesses, the home computer market, and schools. The power of the Web lies in its ability to:

1. present information in a nonlinear format, allowing the user to access the information in a nonlinear, nonsequential fashion
2. include all types of information—anything that can be digitized
3. link one document to another, all on the same screen
4. highlight certain words (concepts, names, etc.) within a paragraph as links to other Web pages
5. allow users to easily share information by constructing home pages
6. offer easy point-and-click navigation
7. present information graphically in a colorful, attractive, and effective fashion
8. to be interactive—enter text, fill out forms, select options, run programs, play sounds, etc.

All of these features support students in the learning process. The Web offers an excellent environment for interactive learning, collaborative learning, exploring, publishing, locating information, and discussion. All of these will be explored further in the chapters on curriculum integration and the Internet.

The Web is very appealing visually, but its popularity lies in its ability to transport the user to other Web pages and other parts of the Internet so seamlessly. It accomplishes this task through a common computer language called Hypertext Markup Language (HTML). Web pages usually contain several, sometimes hundreds, of connections called *hyperlinks*. When clicked on, these hyperlinks take the user to another place on the same Web page or to a totally different Web page altogether. Hyperlinks can be linked to images, or they can activate the transfer of digital information such as video or audio clips. They can take the user to a place outside the Web, such as gopher or a telnet location, or they can call an e-mail window to send a message. There is no one set path when reading hypertext; the user determines which link to click on next. Hypertext information is organized as an interconnected web of linked information (text, graphics, sound, etc.). This allows different readers to follow different paths through the same information. One way to understand hypertext is to think of it as a metaphor for the way the human mind works. As we think, one idea is connected to another and then to another in random, unstructured patterns but with some loose relationship to each other. On the Web, a hyperlink connects one page to another page in a pattern somewhat similar to a spider's web.

IN THE BEGINNING

The Internet started originally as Advanced Research Projects Agency Network (ARPANET), a project created by the Department of Defense to carry information to defense contractors. It was developed to function even under an enemy attack. A method was devised to route information through many interconnected systems to get to the final destination. When the packets of information couldn't get through one line, they would be automatically routed to another. This is what makes the Internet so viable today. In the 1980s the National Science Foundation created NSFnet, based on this model but with higher-speed communications, allowing government agencies, scientists, and researchers to communicate. As access became easier, a more diverse group of people across the world became involved. Now people from K–12 education, both children and adults, log onto the Internet daily.

TIP

Robert Hobbes' Zakron's Internet Timeline is a list of significant events in Internet history spanning the time from 1957 to present.

http://info.isoc.org/guest/zakon/Internet/History/HIT.html

For more in-depth information on the history of the Internet, see Netizens: On the History and Impact of Usenet and the Internet.

http://www.columbia.edu/~hauben/netbook/

Today the Internet is many, interconnecting networks funded by both commercial and government organizations encompassing networks in over 250 countries. Since its creation the Internet has grown exponentially in terms of the number of networks now connected to it and the amount of information being transferred. According to Mark Lottor of Network Wizards in Menlo Park, California, there were 6,642,000 hosts in July 1995; only 24 months later there were 16,146,000. Trying to estimate the number of Internet users is like trying to hit a very complex and moving target. The latest figures estimate that approximately 29 million people over the age of 16 are on the Internet.

TIP

If you need current Internet statistics for reports or presentations to parents, the Library of Congress Web page, Internet Statistics, contains a large collection of Web sites that collect Internet statistics.

http://lcweb.loc.gov/global/internet/inet-stats.html

The growth of the World Wide Web has been remarkable, even compared to the Internet at large, as shown by the number of hosts per Web server. Matthew Gray at MIT recorded its growth from December of 1994, with only 130 Web sites, to 100,000 in January of 1996. See the Web site at http://www.mit.edu/people/mkgray/net/. As of May 1997, there are over 8,000 school Web sites registered on Web66, http://web66.coled.umn.edu/schools/stats/stats.html.

TIP

For more detailed reports on school Internet access see the National Center for Educational Statistics Web site at http://NCES.ed.gov/pubs/ 97944.html or ETSnet at http://www.ets.org/research/pic /comp-class.html. The Library of Congress offers links to sites that maintain general Internet statistics at http://lcweb.loc.gov/global/internet/ inet-stats.html.

An interesting way to monitor Internet growth is by the Internet Index, maintained by Win Treese at Open Market. Based on the famous "Harper's Index," published in *Harper's Magazine,* the Internet Index describes itself as "an occasional collection of facts and statistics about the Internet and related activities." In addition to gaining insight about the Internet, it's amusing (http://www.openmarket.com/intindex/).

July 1996

Number of states with organized programs for schools on NetDay'96: 27

Estimated size of Internet access market in 1997, in billions of dollars: 2.5

Number of private Internet providers in Egypt: 7

Percentage of online users in the San Francisco Bay area who are female: 47

February 1997

Number of times President Clinton mentioned the Internet in the 1997 State of the Union address: 6 times

Number of times he mentioned it in the 1996 address: 0

Number of State of the Union addresses carried live on the Internet: 1

Approximate number of new domain name registrations, per month: 85,000

Number of people who worked on the NFL's Super Bowl Web site: 35

April 1997

Number of priests in *Catholic Priest On Line* on AOL: 30

Estimated number of jobs created by the Internet in 1996, worldwide: 1.1 million

Number of subscribers to the A.Word A. Day mailing list: 68,355

Percentage of ads containing URLs in the first 20 pages of *Good Housekeeping* (March 1997): 54

Number of mailing lists in the liszt.com directory: 71,618

ADVANCED STRATEGY

For an insightful explanation of the history of planning and decision making for the information highway, logon to Andy Carvin's EdWeb at http://edweb.gsn.org/ibahn/index.html.

WHO OWNS THE INTERNET?

No one owns the Internet or, more accurately, "nobody and everybody." The various networks that make up the Internet have their own governing body, usage policies, and owners. These include NSFnet, that is funded publicly and CERFnet, that is privately funded. The one group that comes the closest to "running" the Internet is the Internet Society or ISOC. It's a nonprofit organization whose purpose is to facilitate and support the technical evolution of the Internet as a research and education tool. Volunteers freely give their time to support and promote the aims of the Internet. ISOC has committees and working groups that establish protocols and standards. The Internet Society, http://www.isoc.org/home.html, publishes a newsletter, the *Internet Society News,* that provides news about Internet development.

The Internet Architecture Board (IAB), which is responsible for ratifying standards (such as protocols and technologies) has numerous committees and working groups. The Internet Engineering Task Force (IETF), specializing in the development and approval of specifications that become Internet standards and the Internet Research Task Force (IRTF), which concentrates on developing technologies that may be needed for the future, both report to the IAB. This sense of cooperation is what the Internet is all about. It is self-governing through a process of cooperative democratic participation. (See Figure 2.2.)

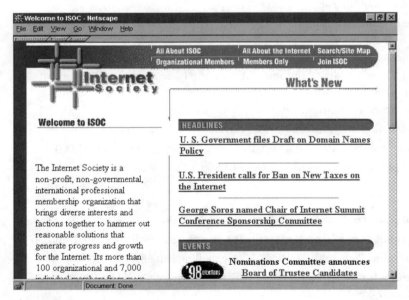

Figure 2.2
Home page for the Internet Society.

There are a few other organizations you should know about that in one way or another play a role in cyberspace.

Farnet. Established in 1987 as the Federation of American Research Networks, its mission is national advocacy, to promote education and research in a network environment. The association offers educational programs and workshops for its members and provides a national forum for discussion of key technical and policy issues. They publish a weekly online newsletter by Harper Boyles, *The Washington Update,* which is available online at http://www.farnet.org/.

The Electronic Frontier.   The Electronic Frontier was founded in July 1990 by Mitch Kapor to make new technologies useful and available to everyone, not just to the techno-logical elite. In keeping with the belief that an individual's constitutional rights need to be preserved in cyberspace, the society places high priority on maintaining the free and open flow of communication. Their Web site is an excellent resource for archived information on civil rights issues on the Net, as well as current battles being fought. Their home page can be found at http://www.eff.org/.

World Wide Web Consortium.   Led by Tim Berners-Lee, creator of the World Wide Web, the W3C is an international industry consortium. It was founded in 1994 to develop common protocols for the evolution of the World Wide Web. You can find the consortium at http://www.w3.org/Consortium/. (See Figure 2.3.)

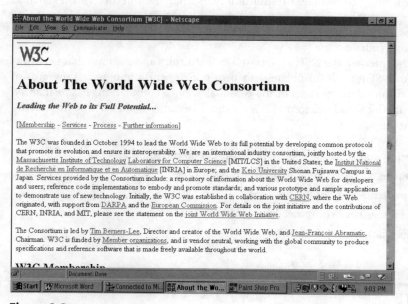

Figure 2.3
Home page for World Wide Web Consortium.

American Library Association (ALA) and American Association of School Librarians (AASL).   Both of these old favorites have Web sites with valuable information for school librarians, such as the Library of Rights, Resolutions on Software Filtering, Acceptable Use Policies for the Internet, and more. Access their Web sites at http://www.ala.org and http://www.ala.org/AASL/.

ADVANCED STRATEGY
Join the Internet Society! Logon on to http://www.isoc.org/member-ship/whyjoin.html and read how you can be part of Internet development and keep current through committee participation, conferences, education, training, and more.

NETIZEN RESPONSIBILITIES

In the past educational institutions were concerned about the commercial use of the Internet. Now the commercial and educational pathways of the Internet have intertwined so much that it is almost impossible (or necessary) to separate the two. Although statements or policies of appropriate use as it pertains to education or business still exist, most people are not as concerned as they once were. Today, appropriate use versus abuse of the Internet focuses on the effective and practical use of the Internet's bandwidth, or the capacity to carry traffic. The growing number of individual, educational institutions, and businesses on the Internet require a higher bandwidth for transmissions. Sometimes a Mirror server, one that contains duplicate data and files, is set up to handle the increased traffic, but Net users, including students, need to be taught responsibility in using the Internet. Abuses such as downloading large graphics files across long distances—just because it can be done—or sending frivolous or questionable e-mail to large mailing lists or newsgroups are ones that students sometimes initiate.

The core of the Internet, the NSFnet, has well-defined rules and assumes that networks interconnected to NSFnet will formulate their own policies and uphold the standards of NSFnet. The Division Advisory Panel of the National Science Foundations has formalized thoughts about unethical and unacceptable activities. In a nutshell, they define these activities as those that purposely:

1. seek to gain unauthorized access to the resources on the Internet
2. waste resources such as people, capacity, or computers
3. disrupt the intended use of the Internet
4. destroy the integrity of computer-based information
5. compromise the privacy of users

NETIQUETTE

As in any community, certain rules and customs evolve to enable everyone to get along and share the resources without negatively affecting each other. The Internet is no different. Rules of conduct usually apply to Internet activities such as e-mail, usenet, and listservs, but other activities also have socially acceptable online behavior. It's important to be aware of these informal rules and guidelines in order to navigate smoothly without negatively impacting others. If you don't follow the rules you may find your mailbox overloaded with unpleasant messages from fellow Net users.

Netiquette is network etiquette, the do's and don'ts of online communication. Some of basic rules in e-mail netiquette when on a listserv or newsgroups include:

- Monitor (or in Internet slang, **lurk**) for a week or two before sending any messages on a listserv or newsgroups. Get a feel for the discussion, the content, and the membership. Check if there is a **FAQ** (frequently asked questions) list before posting questions.
- Don't use all caps—it's considered **SHOUTING**.
- Keep your messages short and to the point. Rambling wastes bandwidth.
- Send private messages to individuals, never to the entire list. This includes "I agree" and "Thank you" messages.
- Don't advertise on lists. That's called **spamming**.
- Avoid sending inappropriate messages, such as practical jokes or chain letters.
- Always cite your sources; respect copyright.
- If you get **flamed**, that is, receive a nasty message, don't react. If it is unjustified, someone else will speak up on your behalf.
- Always fill in the subject line. This allows readers to delete those messages that don't interest them.

TIP
For more detailed information and list of netiquette rules, see Rinaldi's Netiquette page at http://www.fau.edu/rinaldi/netiquette.html or Albion's home page on Netiquette at http://albion.com/netiquette/index.html.

KEEPING UP WITH THE INTERNET

As you learn about the Internet you're going to have many questions. This, unfortunately, is compounded by the Internet's constant evolution. The Internet is always changing; it's never the same for two consecutive days. As soon as you think you have a handle on it, a new, updated version of your favorite browser is released. Your favorite Web site takes a new direction, another adds a different search engine, and still others disappear altogether. But, don't worry, everyone is having the same problem of struggling to learn about a constantly changing electronic environment. There are online resources that offer help both for *newbies* (new users on the Internet) and for experienced Internet navigators.

To locate updated Web sites for beginners, check out the following places.

Yahoo Beginner's Guide at http://www.yahoo.com/Computers_and_Internet/Internet/Information_and_Documentation/Beginner_s_Guides/ is an excellent starting place. This site will give you an overview of what is currently available for beginner's on the Internet. It contains lots of links to lists, tutorials, basic questions and answers, in-depth guides, and more. (See Figure 2.4.)

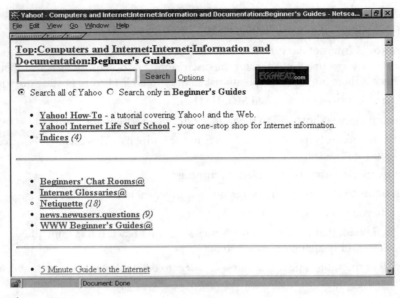

Figure 2.4
If you're an Internet beginner, start at this Yahoo site for help
with navigating the Web.

FAQs (Frequently Asked Questions) at http://www.cis.ohio-state.edu/hypertext/
faq/usenet/FAQ-List.html, contain answers to questions commonly asked by
newcomers to the Net. This collection of FAQs, one of the largest on the Internet,
can be searched by keyword.

Newbie Newz is a newsletter for the new Internet user mirroring the ROADMAP
Interactive Workshop. It features assignments to help new users learn the ins and
outs of FTP (file transfer protocol), Telnet, and WWW and to learn about
resources on the Internet. To subscribe, send an e-mail message to Newbie
Newz-request@IO.COM. In the body of the message type "subscribe
NewbieNewz <your e-mail address>" without the quotes.

For reviews of new Internet resources, and thoughtful commentary on Internet issues
and events, see the following sites.

Scout Report at http://wwwscout.cs.wisc.edu/scout/report is a weekly publication
offering a selection of new and newly discovered Internet resources of interest to
researchers and educators. Located in the Computer Sciences Department at the
University of Wisconsin-Madison, it is sponsored by the National Science
Foundation and is a project of the InterNIC. (See Figure 2.5.)

What's New on Yahoo is at http://www.yahoo.com/new/. The Web announcement page for Yahoo, one of the largest subject lists of Web resources, contains
the latest sites added during the past week.

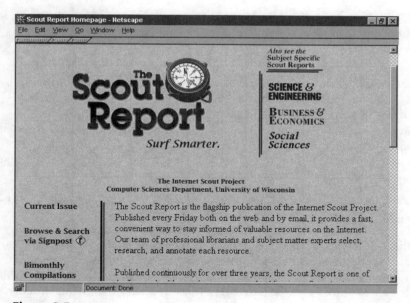

Figure 2.5
The Scout Report helps researchers and educators find new Internet resources.

Net-Happenings, http://www.mid.net:80/NET/, is a popular current events service offering a daily compilation of articles gathered from newsgroups, mailing lists, and other sources. You can access it from the Web site, or you can subscribe to Net-Happenings by sending an e-mail message to listserv@lists.internic.net. In the body of the message type "subscribe net-happenings <your first name your last name>" without the quotes.

Whole Web Catalog, http://features.yahoo.com/zdmicro/web/index.html, includes a Web-Basics section for beginners featuring Internet-related articles from ZDNet magazines, such as *PC Magazine, Internet Week, Internet Life, Computer Life* and more.

 ICONnect is a good place to start if you are new to the Internet. Go to the ICONnect Web site and sign up for a free online introductory course on the Internet, IBASICS. Learn how to use a Web browser, how to e-mail, join a listserv, and more. (See the Preface for the ICONnect Web site address.)

Current Cites, an annotated monthly bibliography of selected articles, books, and electronic documents on information technology is available on the Web and as a listserv. To subscribe to the listserv, send the message "sub cites <your name>" to listserv@library.berkeley.edu, without the quotes.

NetGuide, http://www.netguide.com/, the online version of *NetGuide Magazine* is chock-full of product reviews, technical tips, and articles focusing on what's new on the Web.

Edupage, a summary of news about information technology, is provided three times a week by EduCom at http://www.educom.edu/web/pubs/edupage.html. EduCom is a nonprofit consortium of higher education institutions that facilitates the introduction, use, and access to and management of information resources in teaching, learning, scholarship, and research. Although it is directed at higher education, many of its resources are helpful for K–12. To subscribe to Edupage send mail to listproc@educom.unc.edu. Include the message "subscribe edupage <your name>" without the quotes.

As you are navigating the Internet, you will come across words, acronyms, and phrases you don't understand. Try these resources—they might help.

Netlingo at http://www.netlingo.com is a dictionary of Internet terms. This site contains definitions of hundreds of words that are emerging as a new vocabulary surrounding the technology and community of the Internet and the World Wide Web. This resource's purpose is to chart a lexicon specific to the digital frontier, reflecting and serving the unique cyberculture. (See Figure 2.6.)

Glossary of Internet Terms at http://www.matisse.net/files/glossary contains a comprehensive glossary of Internet terms that can be downloaded for noncommercial, educational use.

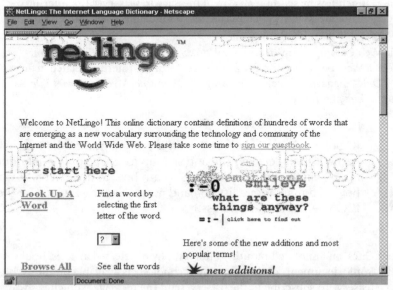

Figure 2.6
Can't figure out an Internet term? Look it up at the Netlingo site.

BABEL: A Glossary of Computer Oriented Abbreviations and Acronyms at http://www.access.digex.net/~ikind/babel.html contains abbreviations and acronyms pertaining to personal computers, multimedia, communications, programming, networking, etc.

The Internet is easy to use, but sometimes it is hard to learn. Even though the World Wide Web has made it easier and more fun to navigate and locate information, it still takes time to understand the Internet. As you locate information, download files, join listservs, be sure to bookmark your favorite sites. Keep a notebook or a log of your journey. The Internet is a place where people support each other, so share your observations and thoughts with others along the way, especially with other educators who are using the Internet. As you network, reflect on your experiences and begin to understand something of what it is and how it works. You'll start to understand the potential for using the Internet in the teaching and learning process.

Chapter 3

Using Internet Tools

Navigating through and locating information on the Web are two of the most talked about and popular computing activities. They are, however, some of the most difficult tasks to accomplish successfully. The Web, an open-ended system combining informational and instructional technology, is unstructured and unwieldy. It is very different from the organized, catalogued collection of information resources students have been trained to use. Currently, there is not a large body of research showing how students search the Web, what skills they need to successfully retrieve information, and how library media specialists can assist and support students in finding the information they need. What little information we have, though, points to the importance of students' critical thinking and problem-solving abilities along with knowledge of the system.[1]

Searching the Web using search engines or directories is a recursive activity. The path is not straightforward, but is instead a constant reevaluation of options and reflection on previous actions. Students' abilities to handle the unstructured environment of the Web relies heavily on their problem-solving and critical thinking abilities, such as scanning, questioning, hypothesis generating, and decision making. These abilities should be taught within the context of the curriculum and practiced and honed through many searching experiences. Learning how to locate relevant information and effectively is an important part of becoming information literate.

Students successfully develop search strategies when they have a mental model of the Web, an orientation to what a nonlinear, hypermedia environment looks like, and a basic understanding of Web browsers, the software necessary to navigate the Web. Successful searchers are aware of the nuances of search engines and have an arsenal of strategies to try.

This chapter presents the basics of Web navigation and information searching. It introduces the Web as an information resource. Students need to understand the Web as an information system with unique characteristics and peculiarities. This understanding only comes from multiple and varied experiences in all different curriculum areas. School Library Media Specialists should develop curriculum activities that ask students to search for information to be evaluated and to be conscious of the strategies the students are using. As students develop an orientation to the Web, form mental models, and learn effective search strategies, they will become information literate.

WEB BROWSERS

A browser's main function is to interpret hypertext documents, read Uniform Resource Locators (URL), and navigate the Web's structure of hyperlinks. Since the first browser, Mosaic, was introduced in 1993, software developers have continued to push Internet technology to the edge, making it easier and more powerful to navigate the Web.

There are two kinds of browsers: text-only browsers and graphical browsers. Text-only browsers can't display graphics and are used by schools that have a low bandwidth. Due to the popularity and growth of the Web as a publishing medium, graphical browsers are the norm. The two major graphic browsers, Netscape Communicator and Microsoft's Internet Explorer, present a variety of information formats on one screen or "page" including sound, video, text, and interactive graphics. Both of these browsers are free to educators: Internet Explorer is free to everyone and Netscape Communicator is free to anyone who qualifies as an educational user. Netscape defines an educational user as "All students from kindergarten to graduate school; Faculty and staff at K–12, colleges and universities; Public Libraries; State departments of education." You can download Netscape Communicator from the Netscape Web site at http://home.netscape.com. If you download the current release it won't expire; if you download the latest Beta version, it will expire in 90 days. When your version expires you can download another at no charge or switch to the current release. The latest version of Internet Explorer, free to anybody, can be downloaded from the Microsoft Web page at http://microsoft.com. Both Netscape and Microsoft will continue to release updates for their browsers, adding new features and altering existing functions. This chapter will present the basics of navigating and using a Web browser.

ADVANCED STRATEGY

Keep up-to-date on the latest browser releases at Browser Watch, http://browserwatch.internet.com/. Encourage students to download new browser releases and evaluate the new functions for library and classroom applicability. Will any of the new functions particularly benefit students or faculty when researching and navigating the Web and constructing Web sites? Have them share their findings on the school library home page.

SOME IMPORTANT TERMINOLOGY TO KNOW

BOOKMARK An electronic marker to a Web page.

BROWSER Software that allows users to access and navigate the World Wide Web.

HOME PAGE The first or introductory page of a Web site. Also referred to as a Web page or Web site.

HTTP (Hypertext Markup Language) Coding language used to create hypertext documents to be posted on the World Wide Web.

IMAGE MAP A graphic that contains hyperlinks.

HYPERLINK A "connector" that links you to another item on the Web when you click on highlighted words or special graphics.

URL (Uniform Resource Locator) Addressing scheme used to identify World Wide Web sites.

WEB Short for the World Wide Web.

WORLD WIDE WEB A revolutionary Internet browsing system that allows for point-and-click navigation on the Internet. Web documents use hypertext, which incorporates text and graphical links to other documents.

How to Use Web Browsers

Most Web browsers function in the same manner. When you begin running the program, the current or default home page appears. This window behaves like any other window on a Mac or Windows computer: it can be opened, closed, resized and moved around the screen. Scroll bars on the right side and the bottom of the window allow you to view parts of the page that are not currently visible. (See Figure 3.1.)

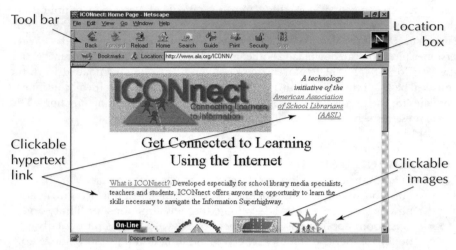

Figure 3.1
The ICONnect Web Page showing the toolbar, location/address box, directory buttons, clickable image, and clickable hypertext link.

How to Read a Web Address

The Web is made up of millions of host computers around the world. Each one has a unique address, a URL. Uniform Resource Locators are similar to e-mail addresses, but they include additional information that make them more powerful.

A Web address reads

   http ://www.ala.org/ICONN/xindex6.html

The first part of the URL identifies the protocol necessary to retrieve the file: *http* stands for Hypertext Transfer Protocol.

   http://*www.ala.org* /ICONN/

The second section is the domain name of the machine on which the file is found. In this case, *ala.org* stands for the American Library Association.

   http://www.ala.org/*aasl/ICONN/*

The last part of the URL specifies the path file name for this page. It's in a directory called *aasl* and a sub-directory called *ICONN* .

By understanding the parts of a URL, students can guess the origination of a Web page, which is a handy skill to have when evaluating an information resource and when fixing an incorrect address.

Moving Around on the Web

To move around the Web, click on a link—an icon, an image, or a highlighted or underlined word. Each of these links contains Internet location information that serves as an address of a Web site. When you click on the link with your mouse, another page of information appears with links to more Web sites. The entire Internet is linked in this manner. Another way to visit destinations on the Web is to type in an address directly in the address box. (See Figure 3.2.)

Figure 3.2
To reach a Web site, type the address in the Location box as shown here. Then hit Enter.

TIP
If you are sent a URL via e-mail, you can copy and paste it into the address box. Highlight the URL in the e-mail message, go to Edit, and click on Copy. Open your Web browser, place the cursor in the address box, go to Edit, and click on Paste.

Netscape Communicator

Netscape Navigator, the browser section of Netscape Communicator, has three toolbars: Navigation toolbar, Location toolbar and Personal toolbar. By selecting View on the menu bar, you can choose to Hide or Show these toolbars. You can minimize and maximize each toolbar by clicking once on the far left end of the toolbar. (See Figure 3.3.)

Figure 3.3
The Netscape Navigator Navigation toolbar.

To move forward or backward, click on the Back or Forward buttons. When information is transferring between the browser and the Internet server you are communicating with, comets and stars are flying past the white N in the upper-right hand corner of the toolbar (or in older versions, the "N" pulses). To stop a transfer in progress, click on the Stop button. You can link directly to a Web site by typing the URL in the Location box and then pressing Enter. Another way to enter a URL is to open the File menu and choose Open Page to bring up a textbox.

TIP
If you want to browse quickly, turn off the automatic image loading by selecting option/Auto Load Images. Placeholders will be substituted for images on the pages you browse.

Click the Search button on the toolbar to display a page offering access to Internet search engines and for other search services (search engines are explained later in this chapter). For additional Internet exploration, click on the Guide button to display a pop-up menu listing Internet directory items. These directories can guide you to various sites and services. Click on the Reload button to redisplay the current page, reflecting any changes made since the original loading. The Security button lets you view and interact with elements such as encryption status, personal and site certificates, security-related applications and passwords.

TIP
If you want to go back many pages easily, use the Go menu rather than clicking many times on the Back button. Repeatedly clicking on the Back button forces your browser to load each page, which is a waste of time.

To print information on the page, select Print on the toolbar. Click on the Home button to return to the current or default home page. A dialog box lets you select print characteristics.

When you want to open your browser, it must open to a location. You can change the default—the Netscape Home page—by clicking on Edit, then Preferences, and then choosing one of three options: open up to a blank page, the last page visited, or a home page which you specify in the box. There are other choices you can make, such as fonts, color, languages, etc., rather than accept the default values. (See Figure 3.4.)

Microsoft Internet Explorer

Internet Explorer has a design similar to Netscape Navigator; however, some terminology is different. Netscape and other browsers use the term *link*, Microsoft calls it a *shortcut*. Microsoft calls saved URLs *Favorites*; others call it *Bookmarks*. Microsoft refers to *pictures*, others, *images*. Microsoft refers to *refreshing* a page; others call it *reloading* a page.

Microsoft Explorer, similar to Netscape, can be personalized for easy access to your favorite sites. You can change the size and position of the toolbar, if you want more screen space to view Web sites, or you can combine all three toolbars, address, command, and links into one.

When Microsoft Explorer is actively transferring information, the letter e with an orbiting disc is circling in the upper right corner of the screen. Personal preferences can be made by going to the View menu and clicking on Options. Choose the home page you want the program to open to. Then change the fonts, color, languages, how long to archive pages in the history folder, the size of your temporary folder, and more. (See Figure 3.5.)

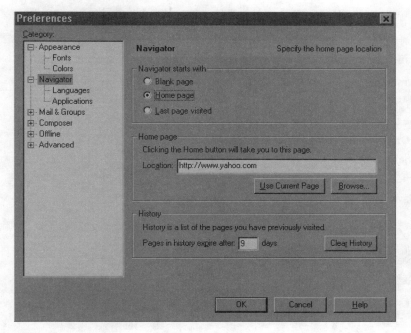

Figure 3.4
A Netscape Navigator Preferences box.

Figure 3.5
The Microsoft Internet Explorer toolbox.

ADVANCED STRATEGY

When you come across a good curriculum site, send it to faculty members that you think would be interested. Open the File menu and choose Send Page. It will automatically have the URL of the current site in the body of the message. Type in your colleagues' e-mail address, add a personal note, and send it.

HOW TO SAVE DOCUMENTS AND IMAGES

As you navigate through the Internet, you will want to save documents as well as print them out. You have the option to save a Web page as a text document or an HTML document. The difference is that the text document will open in your word processor and the HTML document will open in your browser. If you want to save a group of web pages or an entire Web site, then it is better to use Web Whacker, a program designed to save multiple Web pages with links, rather than the Save function. Chapter 8 explains Web Whacker and how to use it.

To save a document, complete the following steps. See Figure 3.6 for specific points.

1. Open File menu.

2. Select Save As.

3. Type in the file name (A).

4. Open the Drives Menu and select a drive and folder (B).

5. Open the Save as Type (C).

6. Select Plain Text (D).

7. Click on Save (E) to save the document.

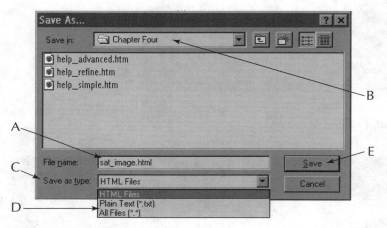

Figure 3.6
Follow the steps to save a document on the Internet.

To save an image, complete the following steps.

1. Position the cursor on the graphic you want to save.

2. Click the right mouse button. See Figure 3.7.

3. Select Save Image as in the pop-up menu box.

4. Type a file name in the Menu box (A). See Figure 3.8.

5. Open the Drives Menu and select a drive and folder (B).

6. Click on Save to save the image (C).

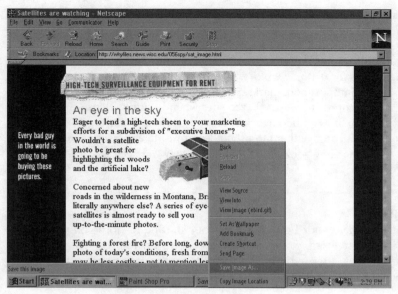

Figure 3.7
Click on the right mouse button to open up a menu. Choose Save an image.

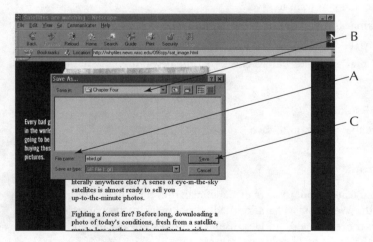

Figure 3.8
Follow the steps to save an image on the Internet.

BOOKMARKS IN NETSCAPE COMMUNICATOR

An electronic bookmark does the same thing a regular one does—it saves your place. It provides fast and easy access to your favorite Web sites. Saving a bookmark is accomplished by accessing a Web page with Netscape, pulling down the Bookmarks menu, and clicking on Add a Bookmark. The title of the Web page is added to the bottom of the Bookmarks menu, and Netscape memorizes the URL associated with the page. The next time you want to access your bookmarked page, just pull down the Bookmark menu, click on the title of the page, and Netscape reconnects right there.

You will find your Bookmarks more and more helpful as you work with students and faculty and recommend sites for them to explore. It is equally important for students to learn how to organize, save, and import bookmarks. Searching is a recursive activity, and students will need to refer back to previously visited Web sites when locating relevant information sources. Teaching students how to bookmark is one way to help them organize and keep track of their resources. Encourage them to use folders for different assignments and projects. If they want to use the same bookmark file at home, they will need to learn how to save their bookmark file.

TIP
You can have your Bookmarks as your starting or home page when you open Netscape. Go to the Edit menu on the toolbar, choose Preferences, then type in the location of the Bookmark file in the Location box.

To Create a Bookmark

1. Go to the Web site that you want to save.
2. Click on the Bookmarks menu on the Location toolbar.
3. Select Add Bookmark.
4. Click on the Bookmarks menu again to check that the new bookmark has been added.

A Shortcut to Create a Bookmark

1. Go to the Web site that you want to save.
2. Click on the right mouse button.
3. Select Add Bookmark.

Bookmarks are a great feature, but to be truly beneficial, they need to be reorganized. As you navigate through the Web, you will undoubtedly bookmark many pages. As the list grows longer it becomes more unwieldy and less useful without some organization. How to delete, copy, or change the name of a bookmark is important.

To Edit Bookmarks

1. Click on the Bookmarks menu on the Location toolbar.
2. Select Edit Bookmarks. A list of your bookmarks will appear in a new window.
3. Use the scrollbar on the right-hand side of the box to view all the bookmarks.

Change the Name of a Bookmark

1. Select the bookmark you want to edit by clicking on it once with your mouse.
2. Open the Edit menu and then select Bookmark properties.
3. Delete the given title and type in the information you want in the Name box.

4. Add comments in the Descriptions box. (Do not change the information in the Location box.)

Delete and Copy Bookmarks

1. Highlight or hold down the CRTL key to select several bookmarks.

2. Open the Edit menu and select Delete, Cut, or Copy.

As your list of bookmarks grows, add order to it by grouping the bookmarks by topic or curriculum area. This can be done by creating new folders and "dragging and dropping" the bookmarks into these folders. The result is a series of cascading menus.

To Organize Bookmarks

1. Click on the Bookmarks menu on the Location toolbar.

2. Select Edit Bookmarks. A list of your bookmarks will appear in a new window.

3. Use the scrollbar on the right-hand side of the box to view all the bookmarks.

4. Open the File menu and select New Folder.

5. Type in the name of the new folder in the Name box.

6. Describe the contents of the folder in the Descriptions box.

7. Click OK when finished.

To Put Bookmarks in a Folder

1. Highlight the bookmark you want to move.

2. Hold down the mouse button and drag the item over to the folder you wish to drop it in. Release the mouse button.

To move a folder, drag and drop in the same way. To open and close a folder, double click on the folder icon. Remember, you can also add a folder to a folder. As an example, create a folder for Social Studies. Then within that folder, create separate ones for American History and European History. Within American History, you can create other folders for Primary and Secondary Sources and so on.

To Save Bookmarks

1. Click on the Bookmarks menu on the Location toolbar.

2. Select Edit Bookmarks.

3. Open the File menu.

4. Click on Save As.

5. Enter the name of the bookmark file in the File Name box.

6. Click on Save.

To Import a Bookmark File

1. Click on the Bookmarks menu on the Location toolbar.

2. Select Edit Bookmarks.

3. Open the File menu.

4. Select Import.

5. Enter the name of the bookmark file in the File Name box.

6. Click on Open.

ADVANCED STRATEGY
There are a few specialized programs called *bookmark utilities* that are designed just for managing bookmarks. Try a 30-day trial copy of First Floor Smart Bookmarks at http://www.firstfloor.com/eval.html. An evaluation copy of Netscape's SmartMarks can be accessed at http://search.netscape.com/home/add_ons/smrtmrks1_0_release.html.

HELPER APPLICATIONS AND PLUG-INS

Even though Web browsers are state-of-the-art Internet technology and are constantly being updated, they cannot handle every type of file found on the Internet. Some audio files, images, video clips, and other multimedia elements cannot be viewed within a Web browser. In such situations you will need to use a *helper application*. A helper application is a program that can display a particular type of file, usually images, movies, and sound clips. Your Web browser launches it, but it is not part of the browser. It is configured to open automatically when it encounters a particular type of file. Helper applications are available on the Web and are either free or offered as shareware. Shareware allows you to try the program for a trial period before purchasing it.

One of the best Web sites for Windows95 users to find helper applications is http://www.winfiles.com/apps/98/multimedia.html. This site maintains an extensive list of downloadable software. Another page of popular helper applications is maintained by the University of California at San Diego, http://ssdc.ucsd.edu/dt/helper.html. Yahoo also maintains a listing at http://www.yahoo.com/Computers_and_Internet/Internet/World_Wide_Web/Browsers/Helper_Applications/.

Two common helper applications are Paint Shop Pro and Cool Edit. Paint Shop Pro handles many different graphic formats and can be found at http://www.jasc.com/. Cool Edit is a sound player and editor for Windows95 and can be downloaded from http://www.syntrillium.com/cool.htm.

Just as helper applications allow you to view file types that are not directly supported by a browser, plug-ins take the concept one step further. Helper applications work separately from your browser, displaying the file contents in a separate window. Plug-ins work seamlessly with your browser. Once installed, the plug-in works automatically. Many plug-ins have educational applications.

Following are a few common plug-ins along with Web sites that show examples of the plug-in.

Adobe Acrobat Reader lets you read electronic documents.
    http://www.adobe.com/prodindex/acrobat/readstep.html
After you download the Adobe reader, visit Larry Anderson's National Center for Technology Planning Web site and download the "Guidebook for Developing and Planning Effective Instructional Technology Plans."
    http://www.nctp.com.

RealAudio lets you listen to live audio feeds over the Internet.
    http://www.realaudio.com
After you download the RealAudio plug-in, visit the National Public Radio site at
    http://www.npr.org and listen to Today's Highlights.

Macromedia's Shockwave plug-in allows you to view movies made with Shockwave.
> http://www.macromedia.com/Tools/shockwave/index.html.

To see how Shockwave is being used on the Web, go to
> http://www.macromedia.com/ Tools/Shockwave/Gallery/index.html.

Inso's Word Viewer Plug-in allows you to view Microsoft Word 6.0 and 7.0 documents with Netscape.
> http://www.software.com/Business_and_Productivity/Microsoft_Office/Word
> _Add_Ons/Review2_4973_index.html

Ichat allows you to go to a Web site and chat, text based, online.
> http://www.ichat.com

HyperStudio, gives you the ability to view HyperStudio projects on the Web without downloading them.
> http://www.hyperstudio.com/lab/plugin.html

The HyperStudio Web site has examples of student work.
> http://www.hyperstudio.com.

Netscape lists plug-ins.
> http://search.netscape.com/comprod/products/navigator/version_2.0/plugins/"

Additional plug-ins for Windows95, Windows 3.x, and Macintosh can be found at CNET's shareware Web site.
> http://www.shareware.com/ and TUCOWS at http://www.tucows.com/.

To follow the development of new plug-ins, go to Browser Watch-Plug-In Plaza.
> http://browserwatch.internet.com/plug-in.html

HOW TO LOCATE INFORMATION ON THE WEB USING SUBJECT DIRECTORIES AND SEARCH ENGINES

Search engines and subject directories help you locate information on the Internet. Although they are becoming similar, there are still distinct differences between the two. A directory is a subject tree or catalog. It organizes the Web by dividing it into topics and subtopics, such as Arts, Sciences, Business, Home, News, and Entertainment. If you are looking for information that fits neatly into a category, then using a directory (such as Yahoo) is the best approach. A search engine is an index that allows you to search on specific words and phrases. You can do a powerful keyword search and a narrower nitty-gritty search of a large number of Web sites using the AltaVista search engine. As a general rule, the more specific the information you need, the more likely you will want to use a search engine.

Subject Directories

Compile sites through human intervention.

Better for broad topics.

Uses directory and sub-directory menus.

Helpful to see broader content of subjects.

Search Engines

Compile sites through computer robots and spiders.

Better for specific information.

Uses keywords and Boolean operators.

More up-to-date and larger than directories.

Subject Directories

Often, students have only a vague idea of the topic they want to research. At this early stage it is difficult for them to identify relevant keywords to effectively employ a search engine. A better strategy is for them to use a subject directory such as Yahoo or Britannica. When using Yahoo with students, encourage them to "drill down" the subject directories starting with the top level. They can also type in "indices" and their topic to locate Web sites that contain lists of Web sites.

Yahoo was one of the first Internet subject directories and is still one of the most popular. To connect to Yahoo, point your browser to http://www.yahoo.com. The opening screen displays the root directory with 14 broad subject categories listed in alphabetical order ranging from Arts and Humanities to Social Sciences. To drill down, click on a topic that interests you. It links you to another page with more subject headings that are much narrower in scope. Select one of these and then continue to do this until you locate a document. You also have the choice of switching to a keyword search at any time. At the top of the screen, enter your keywords in the box and choose to search either in the subject you are currently in or all of Yahoo's subject categories. (See Figures 3.9, 3.10, 3.11, and 3.12.)

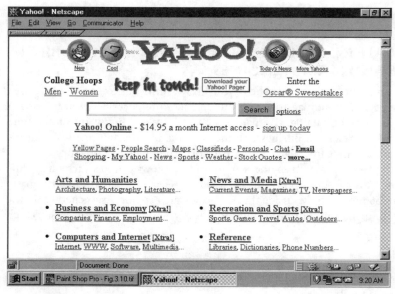

Figure 3.9
To drill down subject directories, first go to the Yahoo home page.

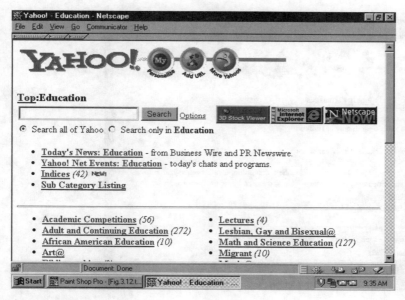

Figure 3.10
Begin with a general topic, in this case, Education.

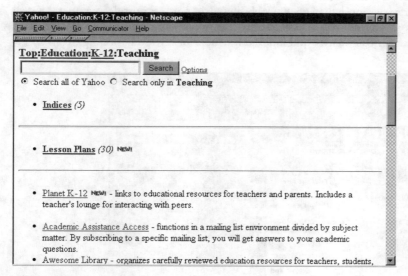

Figure 3.11
Narrow the topic further by looking for Education for K–12,
specifically, Teaching.

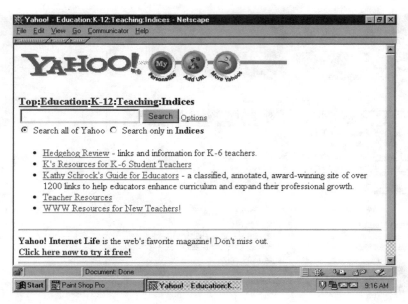

Figure 3.12
Complete the search by using the Indices for specific links.

Two other good subject directories are the Britannica Internet Guide and the Virtual Library. Britannica Internet Guide at http://www.ebig.com is a navigation service that classifies, rates, and reviews more than 65,000 Web sites. Britannica editors deconstruct the Web to identify quality Web resources. These resources are clearly and concisely described, rated according to consistent standards, and indexed for superior retrieval. (See Figure 3.13.)

Figure 3.13
The Britannica Internet Guide, by *Encyclopaedia Britannica,* is another subject directory.

The Virtual Library at http://vlib.stanford.edu/Overview.html is the oldest catalog of the Web, created by Tim Berners-Lee, who also created the Web. It is run by a loose confederation of volunteers who compile pages of key links for particular areas in which they are expert. It doesn't have the same breadth of coverage as Britannica; however, it is very valuable due to the care and expertise that has gone into writing and maintaining the pages. Another valuable resource is the Internet Public Library at http://www.ipl.org. It began in 1995 and has served over 7,000,000 users in more than 135 countries. Its mission is to locate, evaluate, organize, describe, and create quality information resources. (See Figure 3.14.)

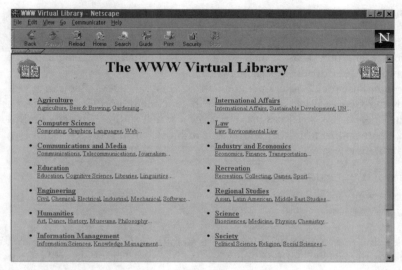

Figure 3.14
The WWW Virtual Library, created by Tim Berners-Lee, is a useful subject directory.

ICONnect
Learn how to search the Internet effectively. Point your browser to the ICONnect Web site to learn about two free online courses: Using Internet and Web Search Engines Effectively, and Advanced Search Strategies. Learn the differences between subject directories and search engines, when to use one over the other, tips and strategies to search effectively, and more.

Search Engines

Search engines use software robots to survey the Web and build their databases. Web documents or sections of Web documents are retrieved and indexed. When you enter keywords or phrases in the search engine, your input is checked against the search engine's keyword indices. The best matches are then returned to you as hits. Search engines get different results on the same searches because they are not searching the Web directly, but rather the database they themselves developed. The degree of detail recorded by search engines varies greatly; some enter the entire text to a searchable field, while others may enter only a short description.

Search engines use a variety of methods and strategies to search the text: keyword searching, Boolean operators, relevance ranking, and refining the search. Review the Help files to learn how that particular search engine works.

Keyword searching is the most common form of text search on the Web. The search engine matches your keywords with its database and returns hits. The results will vary depending on how the database was constructed. Remember to be as precise as possible. Search engines are dumb—they can't differentiate among Venus the planet, Venus the goddess, and Venus the astrological sign. The word "Venus" is just a string of characters to the computer. Students therefore need to be reminded to think carefully. They must analyze results, use Boolean operators and wildcards, and reflect on their search before they click.

Debbie Abilock, Librarian at The Nueva School in Hillsborough, California, describes a creative way to help students develop relevant keywords in an article entitled "The Gestalt of Online Searching" in *Multimedia Schools*.[2] Asking the question: How do words relate to topics? Roy Tennant, Internet expert, searches the Web by thinking of a possible title for a Web document he would like to find. He then goes to a search engine that allows him to limit to titles, phrases, and mixed cases (such as AltaVista) and enters "My Imagined Title Words." It often produces key documents right away.

Most search engines use the Boolean operators AND, OR, NOT, and NEAR. Boolean operators were named after George Boole (1815–1864) who combined the study of logic with algebra. Using the Boolean AND it is possible to narrow a search so that you get a limited number of hits. Another operator, NOT, allows you to block out certain terms, and OR expands your search. An example of each is:

> Anabolic steroids AND sports
>
> Burgundy NOT wine
>
> Cardiac OR heart

Each search engine uses a Boolean operator as default. AltaVista, InfoSeek, and WebCrawler use OR while Excite, Hot Bot, and Magellan use AND. The results will change depending on what operator is used, so it's important to know this before searching.

A wildcard (a word marked with an asterisk) allows you to search simultaneously for several words with the same word stem. A search using "child*" will find documents with "child", "child's" and "children."

Search engines will return results with relevancy rankings, listing the hits according to how close they think the results match the query. The ranking is usually based on the word frequency and where the word is positioned in the document. This sometimes means that it is not necessary to search more than the first few pages even when the total result numbers in the thousands.

Power Search Tips

1. Decide whether you need to use a directory or a search engine. The more narrow the topic, the better to use a search engine.

2. When using a search engine for the first time, take the time to read any instructions, "Tips" files, and FAQs to find out:
   a. What strings it accepts.
   b. Which Boolean operator does it use as the default.
   c. If you have any options in the way the results are presented to you.

3. Understand what you are looking for and know some of the terminology of your target topic. The broader and more ill defined the search query, the more extraneous, useless information you will find. You will learn about your subject as you search, but it's better to have some basic background information on the topic. That way you can narrow the search, be precise, and target the needed information.

4. Run your search on different search engines and compare the results. Don't think all search engines are the same.

5. Don't assume the large, general search engines are always the best. Consider a specialized index such as FindLaw, a database on legal code and case law, at http://www.findlaw.com.

6. When searching for a proper name, capitalize the first letter of each word.

7. Use quotation marks when doing a phrase search.

8. Learn to use a wildcard (an asterisk) to find combinations of words or word fragments.

9. Beware of terms with double meaning. "Chicks" can pull up graphics of scantily clad women as well as baby chickens. "Spiders" can be either computer programs used by search engines or eight-legged arachnids.

10. Often, a search will retrieve links to many documents at one site. Rather than clicking on each URL in succession, truncate the URL at the point that appears most likely to represent the document you are seeking and type this URL in your browser's Location box.

11. Watch your spelling. Misspelling changes search results.

12. Master Boolean logic. All search engines use some form of it to refine searches.

13. Each search engine is different. Decide on your favorite and learn its nuances.

14. If it is not clearly evident why a search engine retrieved a document, use the browser's FIND button to search for the text in the current document.

To help students decide which search engine will help with their information needs direct them to Debbie Abilock's "Choose the Best Search Engine for Your Information Need" at http://nueva.pvt.k12.ca.us/~debbie/library/research/adviceengine.html. (See Figure 3.15.)

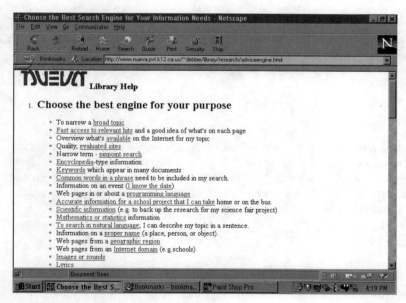

Figure 3.15
The Web site for Debbie Abilock's Advice Engine.

SEARCH STRATEGIES
How do I find information on the Internet? Join a CyberTour to learn some strategies and tips on effective use of search engines and subject directories to satisfy your information needs quickly and efficiently.

Searching on AltaVista

AltaVista is considered to be one of the largest, fastest and the most sophisticated search engines on the Web. It claims to index up to 95 percent of the Web and is updated daily. To begin a search, point your browser to http://www.altavista.digital.com.

Check the Help Files

Before you begin searching, click on the help section of the search engines. AltaVista' s help sections contain the following helpful tips.

1. Use a plus sign for required words, minus sign for words that should be excluded.

2. Capitalization forces a case-sensitive match.

3. Use wildcards for truncation

4. You can limit a search to a specific field:

   Title: "ancient world"

   > (phrase "ancient world" must be in the title)

   url: ibm

   > (word *ibm* must be somewhere in the URL)

   host: digital.com

   > (*digital.com* must be in the host name of the server)

TIP
Bookmark the search engine page containing your key words. When you return, it will refresh the search.

AltaVista has two types of searches: simple and advanced. To run a simple search, enter keywords or any string of letters or digits in the dialog box. AltaVista will retrieve documents matching any of the keywords you entered, listing them in order of relevancy. You can add a plus sign to indicate that the word must be present in the document or a minus sign to indicate that it should not be in the document. (See Figure 3.16.)

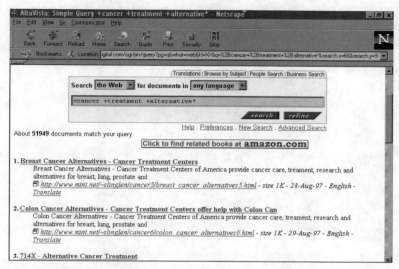

Figure 3.16
An AltaVista search on cancer using plus signs.

Another way to specify your search is to click the Refine button and view a list of words commonly found in the search results. You can refine the search by including or excluding any of those words from a subsequent search. This encourages students to think about the importance of specific words in their search strategy. (See Figure 3.17.) You can also request the results in a graphical format. (See Figures 3.18 and 3.19.)

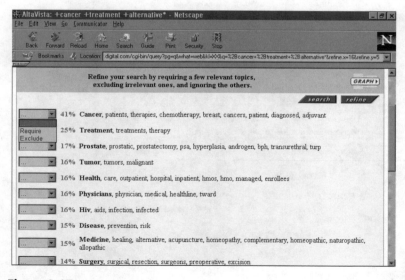

Figure 3.17
An AltaVista search using Refine.

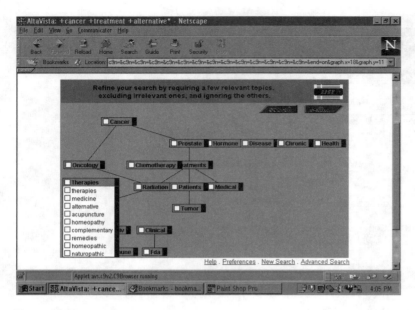

Figure 3.18
An AltaVista search in graphic format.

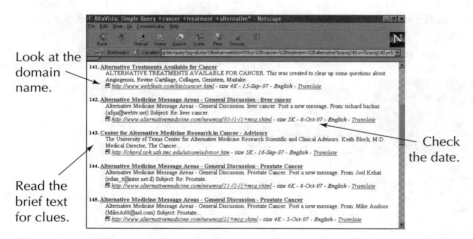

Figure 3.19
How to read AltaVista search results.

Help Students Understand the Search Results

When students retrieve search results they need to learn how to look at the results and decipher relevant information. In addition to the name of the Web page, the citation also includes the URL that gives clues as to whether a company, a branch of government, a university, etc., owns the Web site. It also gives the size of the file and the date.

In addition to AltaVista the major search engines include the following.

Excite http://www.excite.com

HotBot http://www.hotbot.com

InfoSeek http://guide.infoseek.com

Lycos http://lycos.com

Open Text http://index.opentext.com

Web Crawler http://www.webcrawler.com

Northern Light http://www.northernlight.com

Meta Search Engines

The growth in the number of search engines has led to the development of "meta" search tools or, as they are sometimes referred to, "multi-threaded search engines." These search engines allow the user to search multiple databases simultaneously, via a single interface. When they were first developed they did not offer the control available when searching with a single search engine; that, however, is changing. Depending on the meta search you are using, the results can be sorted by type of resource, by site, or by domain. These modifications greatly added to their effectiveness. Examples of these search engines include the following.

Dogpile http://www.dogpile.com

Internet Sleuth http://www.isleuth.com/

MetaCrawler http://www.metacrawler.com

All-In-One http://www.albany.net/allinone

Keeping Up with Search Engines

Modifications of search engines and introduction of new features are constantly being announced. To keep up-to-date on search engines and learn more about them, check out the following resources: Spider's Apprentice, Sink or Swim, and Learning How to Search the Web Theme Page. (See Figures 3.20, 3.21, and 3.22.)

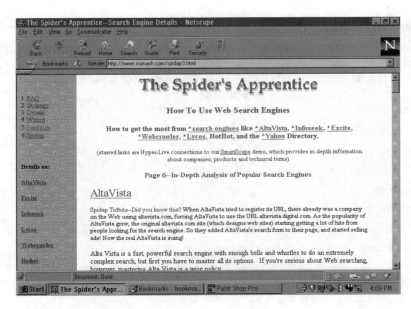

Figure 3.20
Learn more about search engines at the Spider's Apprentice Web site.

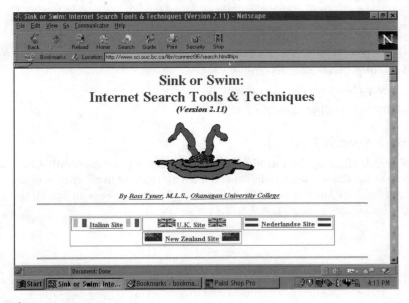

Figure 3.21
This Sink or Swim Web site gives more information about search engines.

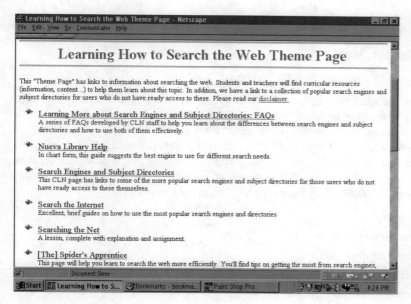

Figure 3.22
Learning How to Search the Web Theme Page will help you . . . search the Web!

ICONnect
Do you have trouble downloading files or navigating the Internet? Do you need help installing and configuring your modem? If you are an AASL member, join TECHDISC, a listserv to help you with your technical and navigation questions. Go to the ICONnect Web site for details on joining TECHDISC. Stop at the AASL Web site at http://www.ala.org/aasl to find out how to become an AASL member.

E-MAIL AND HOW TO USE IT

Electronic mail, or e-mail, is a way of sending an electronic letter or message between individuals or computers through the systems and networks that make up the Internet. E-mail is the most popular of the three traditional Internet applications. Telnet and FTP (file transfer protocol), the other two traditional applications, are usually performed, almost seamlessly, through the Web now. Whether you are on a T1 line connected to the Internet, or use a telephone line to dial with 1,200 baud access to the Internet, you can send an electronic message over the lines. A full Internet connection is not necessary to send e-mail. All you need is a computer, a modem, and a connection to the Internet.

E-mails are composed of three sections: a header, body, signature, and, sometimes, attachments. The header contains the TO—whom you are sending the e-mail message to, the FROM—your name and e-mail address, and the SUBJECT—the topic of the message and transmission data, which will add the date and time you sent the message automatically.

An e-mail address is composed of three sections: username, domain name, and top-domain name. An @ sign separates the user name from the domain name.

> pberger@byramhills.org

> User name@domain name.top-domain name

Your Internet provider usually assigns the user name. It can be a series of letters and numbers, but usually it is some form of the user's name. The domain name describes your Internet server. It is the computer on which the user has an account.

My Compuserve account address reads pberger@compuserve.com. If I worked at a university, it would read pberger@university.edu. The top-domain name is separated by a period and tells you the type of host. Plans are underway to broaden the number of top-level domain names available. (See Figure 3.23.) Here are the old-timers:

.edu university

.com commercial enterprise

.org non-profit organization

.gov government institution

.mil military institution

.net computer network

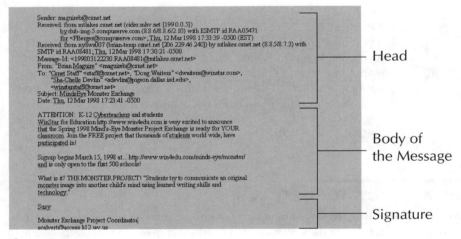

Figure 3.23
Parts of a typical e-mail message.

Most e-mail programs allow you to save signature information, your name, e-mail address, school name and address, etc., in a file that will be added automatically to every e-mail. It's a good idea to set this up for permanent usage rather then type the information each time you send an e-mail message, but try to keep this short. Some people add quotes to the signature file, which is acceptable if it is kept within 5 or 6 lines. It is considered a waste of bandwidth and, therefore, irresponsible to include lengthy quotes, drawings, etc.

TIP
To read about e-mail Netiquette, logon to A Beginner's Guide to Effective e-mail at http://www.webfoot.com/advice/email.top.html.

Using e-mail, you and your students can exchange ideas with people all over the world. You can send and receive files and lesson plans. Or you can correspond with experts and conduct ongoing projects with students in other areas. To locate key pals, logon on the Global School Network at http://www.gsn.org.

E-Mail Tips

1. Type the address carefully. Pay particular attention to the spelling, dots, capitalization, spacing, symbols, etc.

2. Keep your messages short and to the point.

3. Don't use capital letters. That's considered SHOUTING.

4. Sign your e-mail with four or five lines from a signature file.

5. Copy and paste brief sections from the e-mail you are replying to so the other person understands your message.

6. Before you hit the reply button, check to see if the message is going to a group, such as a listserv, or an individual.

Using Smileys and Abbreviations

Because e-mail is believed to be a cold communication medium, lacking in facial, vocal, and body gestures, people have turned to other ways of communicating to smooth out interaction. These written expressions are added to the ends of sentences that may be mildly controversial or could be misinterpreted. Abbreviations, such as IMHO (in my humble opinion) or BTW (by the way), are also used to aid communication. These are a few common ones. There are books devoted to smileys and e-mail abbreviations, if you want to research further. Hundreds of smileys are recorded at http://www.cynet.net/smile.html. To generate a random smiley go to http://www.goldendome.net/Tools/cgi-bin/smiley.cgi. To view the following smileys, tilt your head to the left.

    :-)   a basic smile, expressing happiness or sarcasm

    ;-)   a whimsical smile or "inside joke"

    :-(a frown

    8-)   wearing glasses

LISTSERVS AND HOW TO USE THEM

Listservs, or mailing lists, are special kinds of electronic mail addresses that automatically forward topic-specific discussions to your e-mail. In essence, it is an online discussion group using e-mail to send and receive the messages. There are over 4,000 mailing lists, worldwide, on almost every topic you can imagine. Once you find a subject that you like, such as distance learning or school libraries, you can subscribe to that mailing list and read what others have to say.

There are several types of listservs. There are "open" lists that anyone can join, such as LM_NET, open to all those interested in school libraries. There are also "closed" lists that are open by invitation only, such as ICONCURR, a curriculum/Internet integration discussion, open only to AASL members. Some mailing lists are used for one-way communication. The IBASICS, an ICONnect online course, delivers lessons every week to subscribers. (See Figure 3.24.)

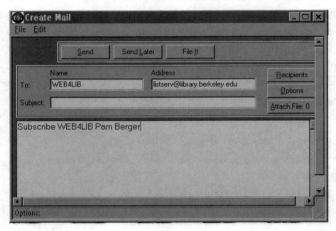

Figure 3.24
How to send e-mail in order to join a listserv.

List software such as Majordomo, ListProc, and Listserv is also available. These all have somewhat different protocols, although the pattern is the same. To subscribe using listserv software, send an e-mail message to the listserv (the computer that controls, sorts, and distributes the messages). As an example, to subscribe to LM-NET, the mailing list for school library media specialists, address the e-mail to listserv@ericir.syr.edu. Leave the subject line blank. In the body of the message, type <Subscribe LM_NET yourfirstname yourlast name>. Send the message. A confirmation or welcome message should come within 24 hours. Save this message because it will contain important information, such as guidelines for subscribers, how to send a message to the list, and how to leave the list. It's important to know that mailing lists have two e-mail addresses: the list address for posting messages and the administrative address you use to subscribe and unsubscribe to the list. Be careful not to send administrative messages to the list address. That's a common mistake that newbies (new Internet users) make.

Following are some tips for using listservs.

1. Start by lurking (reading messages without responding) in order to learn more about the people and the topic of the listserv. This is a good way to find out if the listserv really interests you. Don't lurk forever, though. You should contribute to the conversation once you feel comfortable.

2. Before you ask a question, check the FAQs (Frequently Asked Questions) to see if the question has already been answered. Some listservs have archives that can be searched by keyword.

3. Read your mail regularly and delete messages you don't need. Otherwise the number of messages in your mailbox will overwhelm you.

4. Some listservs will allow you to receive your mail in digest form, which combines multiple messages into a single e-mail. This might help you to manage large amounts of e-mail from listservs.

5. Limit the number of listservs you subscribe to. If you find you are deleting the messages without even reading them, then it's time to remove yourself from the listserv.

How to Find Listservs

Following are several mailing lists of particular interest to school librarians and other educators. In addition, there are several resources for mailing lists. The Directory of Scholarly and Professional E-Conferences at http://www.n2h2.com/KOVACS/ offers you the ability to search for mailing lists and browse the list by name or subject. Another resource is Title.Net http://title.net/listserv/index.html to see lists organized by name, description, subject, and more. For a full listing, go to http://www.liszt.com to search by keyword. Go to http://k12.cnidr.org:90/lists.html for a list of educational-related listservs. There is even a listserv you can join to receive regular notice of new listservs called NEW-LIST@vm1.nodak.edu.

Library/Education Related Listservs

AUTOCAT Important discussion list for cataloging. Send the message <subscribe AUTO-CAT yourfirstname yourlastname> to listserv@listserv.acsu.buffalo.edu

BIGSIX Discussion on the Big Six information literacy skills model. Send a message <subscribe BIGSIX yourfirstname yourlastname> to listserv@listserv.syr.edu

CHILD_LIT Discussion of children's and young adult literature. Send a message <subscribe CHILD_LIT your.email address> to majordomo@mail.rutgers.edu

EDNET Discussion of educational possibilities of the Net. Send a message <subscribe ednet yourfirstname yourlastname> to listproc@lists.umass.edu

EDTECH Devoted to educational technology. Send the message <subscribe yourfirstname yourlastname> to listserv@msu.edu

EDUPAGE An online biweekly newsletter on education and technology. Send the message <subscribe edupage yourfirstname yourlastname> to listproc@listServ.oit.unc.edu

ISED-L Discussion list for independent school faculty, administrators, and parents. Send the message <subscribe ISED-L yourfirstname yourlastname> to listServ@listserv.syr.edu

K12ADMIN K–12 educators interested in educational administration. Send the message <subscribe K12ADMIN yourfirstname yourlastname> to listserv@listserv.syr.edu

KIDLINK Discusses KIDLINK's current year project. Send the message <subscribe KIDLINK yourfirstname yourlastname> to listserv@listserv.nodak.edu

LM-NET The discussion list for school library media personnel. Send a message <subscribe LM_NET yourfirstname yourlastname> to listserv@listserv.syr.edu

MIDDLE-L A discussion for those involved in the education of middle school students. Send the message <subscribe MIDDLE-L yourfirstname yourlastname> to listserv@postoffice.cso.uiuc.edu

NNEWS Online newsletter focusing on Internet library resources. Send the message <subscribe NNEWS yourfirstname yourlastname> to listserv@listserv.nodak.edu

PENPAL A discussion list for those interested in finding individual pen pals. Send the message <subscribe PENPAL-L yourfirstname yourlastname> to listserv%unccvm.bitnet @listserv.net

STUMPERS-1 Difficult reference questions. Send the message <subscribe scribestumpers-1 yourfirstname yourlastname> to mail@serv@crf.cuis.edu

WEB4LIB A discussion for libraries using the web. Send the message <subscribe WEB4LIB yourfirstname yourlastname> to listserv@library.berkeley.edu

WWWEDU A discussion focusing on methods of integrating the WWW into schools. Send a message <subscribe WWWEDU yourfirstname yourlastname> to listproc@ready.cpb.org

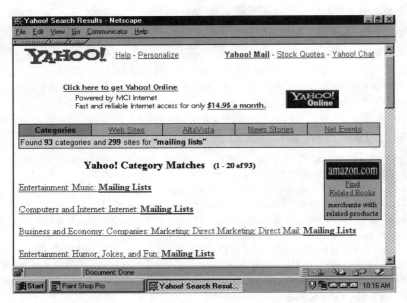

Figure 3.25
Check out this Web site to find different Yahoo mailing lists.

NOTES

1. Delia Neuman, "Current Research," *School Library Media Quarterly* (1997): 229.
2. Debbie Abilock, "The Gestalt of Online Searching," *Multimedia Schools* (1997): 23.

Chapter 4

How to Evaluate Web Sites

Is the author an authority on the subject? Is the work comprehensive? Is there a bias evident? What's the copyright date? These are familiar questions for school library media specialists. We ask them every day when helping students evaluate resources and in selecting resources for our libraries. With the advent of the Web, the urgency to evaluate resources has increased dramatically. School librarians have a unique opportunity to use and adapt their professional evaluation skills to help students and teachers meet the challenge of the information age.

Knowledge continues to double at an increasingly fast rate, as does the number of new web sites. Anyone can publish on the Internet, and the Web is especially easy to do so on. All you need is a computer, an Internet provider, and some knowledge of HTML (hypertext markup language) or a Web authoring program. The material you find on the Web may not be edited, reviewed, or sponsored by an individual or organization that is knowledgeable about the content. In fact, the content may not be accurate at all. Therefore, the need for evaluation is even more important. Urgency for evaluation takes two forms: to teach students how to evaluate Web sites and to evaluate Web sites for inclusion in virtual library web pages. The virtual library page supports the effective integration of Internet resources into the curriculum and the teaching and learning process. In essence, evaluation focuses on collection development and teaching information literacy skills.

EVALUATING WEB SITES FOR COLLECTION DEVELOPMENT

As an informational specialist, you are the most qualified person in the school to evaluate and organize information sources, including electronic resources. Just as you evaluate and select resources for the print, CD-ROM, and video collections, Internet resources need to be evaluated, selected, organized and made available to the school community on a virtual library page.

Teachers, students and parents need guidance in locating Web resources. A math teacher needs to know which Web site will offer the best interactive experiences with geometry theorems; social studies teachers need to incorporate primary sources in a curriculum unit. French teachers want to set up a collaborative project with students in a French-speaking country. A student asks where to get the latest stock quotes and historical information on a few companies; a parent wants information on Web sites addressing learning disabilities.

Neither you nor your students and teachers will have the time to meet and have a lengthy discussion every time they need to access a Web page. Therefore, a virtual library page is essential to the library program. Just as they seek out the online catalog to select books, CD-ROMs, videos, and other resources to support the curriculum or answer a reference question, they will turn to the Library Media Center Virtual Library Page to access relevant, authoritative Web resources. The Web sites on the virtual library page are evaluated and selected by educators, the School Library Media Specialist, and/or faculty, and they follow the guidelines in the school library's collection development policy. The virtual library page site should reflect the curriculum and unique information needs of your school and the teaching and learning process. Additional information on developing a virtual library home page is in chapter 7.

TEACHING STUDENTS TO BECOME INFORMATION LITERATE

The Internet has created an increased awareness of the need to teach students to be information literate. Teaching information skills is not new to school librarians who have guided students to look at the authority and reliability of print resources for years. However, they often did not have the opportunity to help students develop critical information skills. Traditionally, there has been a heavy dependence on textbooks as the primary source of information in the classroom. Many teachers relied solely on lecturing as the only teaching strategy for the duration of the instructional unit. Students were not given the chance to develop the skills necessary to locate and evaluate information relevant to the curriculum and their own information needs. Textbook authors have traditionally decided for students what information is relevant and what is not. For the most part, librarians and parents have chosen books for kids, weeding out the inaccurate and deciding on what was appropriate for their needs. Rarely did students gain access to raw, unfiltered, even contradictory information to test and strengthen information literacy skills. For better or worse, the Web is starting to change that.

As teachers and administrators become aware of the immense amount of resources available on the Web, they also realize the vital role school library media specialists play in helping students and teachers become information literate in an electronic information world. If we expect students to become self-directed, lifelong learners and productive citizens, we need to make sure they are information literate. Students must be able to locate pertinent information, evaluate its reliability, analyze and synthesize the information to construct personal meaning, and apply it to informed decision making.

Teaching students to evaluate Web sites critically is crucial. Unfortunately, many students think that if they find the information on the Web, then it must be true. School librarians or teachers carefully select books, magazines, and other information resources students regularly use, so they have very limited experience with false, erroneous, or strongly biased information. When it comes to computers, they are naïve. Students often ask me in disbelief why someone doesn't patrol the Internet and remove the inaccurate information. I'm delighted when students raise these questions since it provides an opportunity for serious class discussion.

When students are required to evaluate Web sites for use in research papers, projects, or Web page development, teachers should include in the project design a section for students to describe sites that they rejected. Have the students include the reasons why, such as they found the information to be biased in some way or found it to be inaccurate compared to other sources.

WEB EVALUATION GUIDE
How do you evaluate Web sites? Hop onboard a CyberTour to learn how to identify good Web sites for K–12 by visiting some good and some not-so-good sites. Learn some tips and strategies to teach students this valuable twenty-first century skill.

ASKING THE RIGHT QUESTIONS

In evaluating Web sites, it's important to ask the right questions. This is especially true when it comes to evaluating Web sites for use in an educational setting. Think carefully about what makes a Web site useful in a library or classroom environment. Most evaluation tools include items to critique the content, design, and technical and navigation features. That's not enough, though. Educators need to ask more probing questions that relate to the teaching and learning process. Technology is expensive and time-consuming to learn to use effectively within the curriculum. The Web site must justify the expense and time needed to have an effective impact on student learning.

Web sites need to use the unique characteristics of the medium. When using a new medium, it takes time to discover what its unique capabilities are. Until we do so, we tend to use it in the same way we employed a previous medium. The first videos developed for classroom use were repurposed filmstrips. In fact, when CD-ROMs were first introduced, a few strongly resembled filmstrips. They were composed in a linear fashion containing a graphic and a short text paragraph with a sound bit added. With vision and experimentation, developers started to design hypertext programs incorporating full-motion video, graphic, sound, and text. The same paradigm applies for the Web. We need to push the edge of the technology to find out how its unique capabilities can be used to support the teaching and learning process.

Good Web sites for education will offer one or more of the medium's unique features—communication, contribution, or access to unique and timely information. These include the ability to:

- communicate with learners around the world—elementary students e-mailing experts and collaborating with other students via e-mail.
- publish and contribute original information—language arts students submitting their writing to an electronic magazine for middle school students.
- locate information never before available—social studies students researching comprehensive, in-depth company reports for their stock portfolios.
- offer access to current, up-to-the-minute information—science students downloading the latest weather reports and tracking storms as they occur.

Educators need to ask the type of questions that will determine the sites' significance to the teaching and learning process. Does the Web site encourage students to be engaged in the process of learning? How does the Web site impact student learning? How is it different from using textbooks or other resources? Is the information found here more comprehensive or timely than traditional resources? Which of the unique characteristics does it employ? Will this site's unique features contribute to a student's deeper understanding of content or concepts?

Ed's Oasis Web site, funded by AT&T Foundation at http://www.edsoasis.org/guide2.html, identifies six areas to evaluate educational Web sites. They include Online Features/Student Action, Online Features/Interface, Curricular Design, Program Design, Instructional Design, and Instructional Support Materials. Each section is subdivided with statements detailing the concepts and providing hotlinked examples for each. Look at the sites they recommend and bookmark this site to return to often—it's worth the visit. (See Figure 4.1.)

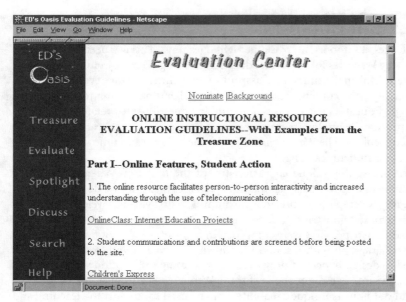

Figure 4.1
When evaluating the usefulness of a Web site, check out Ed's Oasis.

The first question to ask when evaluating a Web site is what is the purpose of the page? Is it to inform, to educate, to entertain, to influence, or to distort? Web pages can be categorized by entertainment, business/marketing/sales, reference/information, news/weather/current events, advocacy, and personal. By identifying the intent of a Web page, it is easier to understand its significance. Jan Alexander and Marsha Tate at the Wolfgram Memorial Library at Widener University's Web page at http://www.science.widener.edu/~withers/webeval.htm provide a teaching module for examining types of Web pages and the unique challenges posed by gathering information on the Web.

Some Web site authors categorize educational pages to make it easier to match the resource to your curriculum need. Blue Web'N Web site, funded by Packbell at http://www.kn.pacbell.com/wired/bluewebn/apptypes.html, identifies six types of educational Web sites. A Tool includes calculators and map generators. A Resource, which does not attempt to be comprehensive, includes magazines, newspapers, books and experts, a hotlist of specialized resources, or a unit or lesson plan. A Reference, which attempts to be comprehensive, includes encyclopedias, dictionaries, and almanacs; and Learning Experiences, which are divided into Lessons, Activities, and Projects. Their Web site has hotlinks to examples of each type by curriculum. While you are there, take some time to explore the entire site and bookmark it. Again, you will want to return often.

The California Instructional Technology Clearinghouse at http://www.clearinghouse.k12. ca.us developed new guidelines designed to provide a single set of rubrics for evaluating all types of instructional technology resources being used in California schools today. The new rubrics, a major departure from the checklists developed in prior years, focus on curriculum content, instructional design, and the needs of the learners for whom the program is intended. The main body of the guidelines is organized into five sections: California Curriculum Content, Instructional Design for Learners, Program Design, Assessment, and Instructional Support Materials. Supplemental Applications Rubrics contains additional rubrics which focus on the unique features of the Web. One for evaluating Web sites is entitled Online Learning Experiences. The rubric is divided into seven sections: online collaboration and communication, navigation, informational content, sharing of learners' work, stability and reliability, new Web features, and instructional support.

ICONnect
Sign up for the ICONnect online course on Web Evaluation specifically designed for K–12 School library media specialists and teachers. It's free and offered a few times a year. All you need is an e-mail account. Instructions are available on the ICONnect Web site at http://www.ala.org/ICONN.

USING A WEB EVALUATION FORM

There are Web evaluation tools available in journals and books and on Web pages that address most of the critical questions about Web sites. They include the following sections:

Authority—Who owns the Web site?

Content—Does the Web site contain accurate, reliable information?

Design and Technical Features—Is the Web site well designed?

Navigation—Can you move around easily and intuitively?

The following Web Evaluation form was first developed for the ICONnect Web site located at http://www.ala.org/ICONN and recently updated. It is designed specifically for evaluating sites for student use in grades K–12 and includes two additional sections usually not found in other evaluation tools: Curriculum Connections and Learning Environment. Curriculum Connections addresses curriculum integration and helps answer the question, How does the Web site support or enhance the teaching and learning process? Learning Environment helps you decide if the site is designed to take advantage of the unique capabilities of the Web (i.e., access to timely or unique information or contribution and communication).

The evaluation tool, reproduced in this chapter, is a guide to help you structure the examination process. It is adapted from the ICONNect Evaluation form. The questions are organized in a logical, sequential order to help you survey the positive features and shortcomings of the Web site. It is designed to help you analyze the true educational value of the Web site and not just the "media glitz." There are many different types of Web sites and no one way to judge all of them. The purpose of the form is to guide you through the evaluation process and teach you to ask appropriate questions. After using the form several times you will develop an intuitive feeling about which Web sites will be successful with your school's curriculum.

Any evaluation is subjective. The Web site is assessed within the general categories outlined in the form, but also according to specific requirements of your school. You need to look at the site with the curriculum, the students, and the teachers in mind. The Web site needs to be developmentally appropriate for the audience. Thus, "meaningful and useful content" depends on who the users are—third graders, eleventh graders, ESL students, or teachers.

While it's impossible to develop a standardized list of questions that can be applied to all Web sites, it is important to consider the sites' unique aspects when looking at them. For example, consider evaluating two different types of educational Web sites, an information resource and interactive site. The information Web site, such as the Library of Congress or the NASA home page, offers access to unique information not available in the school library media center. Therefore, the Content section of the evaluation form will be very important. Whereas, if looking at KidsNews (a Web site that offers students the opportunity to publish), content is not the top priority, but rather Navigation and, of course, Learning Environments.

ICONnect

Do you need an Evaluation Form for your school? Get the latest ICONNect Evaluation Form on the Curriculum Connections section of the ICONnect Web site. Download the entire form or cut and paste sections to meet your instructional needs. Instructions are on the ICONnect Web site. Link to the ICONnect Web site at http://ala.org/ICONN. Click on Curriculum Connections to locate the latest version of the ICONnect Evaluation form. It is updated periodically. Download a copy to your word processor and cut and paste the sections to customize a new form for your instructional needs.

Authority/Credibility: Who owns the Web site and why?

Are the author's name and e-mail address included?

Is the Web site affiliated with any major institutions or organizations?

What is the expertise of the individual or group that created the site?

Does the author's/group's affiliation appear to bias the information?

Is the purpose of the Web site stated?

Is personal information requested from the user?

(See Figures 4.2 and 4.3.)

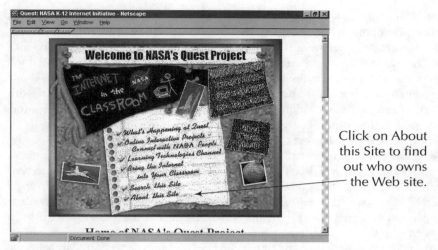

Click on About
this Site to find
out who owns
the Web site.

Figure 4.2
Web site illustrating the Authority aspect. All Web sites should clearly
indicate who is responsible for the content.

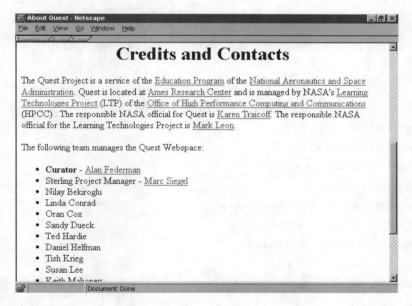

Figure 4.3
Web site illustrating the Authority aspect. This site provides information
on all the institutions, organizations, and individuals responsible for
the Web site.

Find out who's talking. Knowing the educational or occupational background of the creator or compiler of the Web site can help determine the reliability and accuracy of the site and its information. Web page authors should sign their pages with their names and e-mail addresses. They should include a resume, research interests, education, and related job experience that support their credibility. Pages sponsored by larger institutions may only provide an address for a Webmaster, but individual content pages should still be signed with an individual's name and e-mail address. You can e-mail the Webmaster to get the information you need. Be suspicious if none of this information is there.

Do a little detective work. Look at the URL to see if it's an educational site (.edu), a government site (.gov), or a company site (.com). If a "tilde" (the ~ character on the far upper right of the keyboard) is in the URL, it's a sub-directory, most likely an individual's personal home page. If you want to track down and learn the originator's name and host server, go to the InterNic home page at http://rs1.internic.net/cgi-bin/whois. If you are not familiar with the organization, search one of the major search engines or directories to see what you find associated with the organization's name.

The purpose of a Web site should be clearly stated in the opening section. This helps the user determine if the site is useful for them. To examine the objectivity of a page, it is helpful to note if the pages are scholarly or produced for the general public and if they are written/complied by an expert or a novice (such as a student contributor). If the page is intended to present a particular opinion and this is clearly understood, that's fine. The problem arises when the author applies hidden personal prejudices, opinions or thoughts, to the information—then the user needs to verify the information in a second source. Before you explore the hypertext links on a page, look to see where they are located. Are all or most of the links internal? The power and uniqueness of a Web page is the ability to hyperlink to other sources, either for validation, continued discussion, or other opinions. If all the links are internal, check the information in another source.

Content: Does the Web site contain accurate, reliable information?

When was it last updated?

Is the content meaningful and useful?

Does it contain original content?

Is any sort of bias evident?

Does the content appear to be fact or opinion?

Does the information appear to be accurate?

Does it contain primary source material?

Are the links up-to-date?

Are the links annotated? Evaluated?

Do multimedia elements help you understand the content better?

Are the grammar and spelling correct?

(See Figure 4.4)

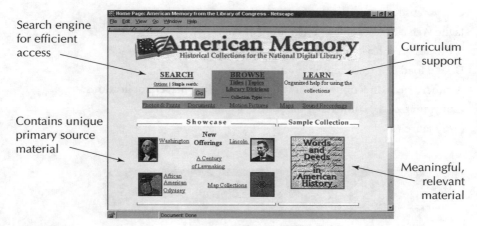

Search engine for efficient access

Contains unique primary source material

Curriculum support

Meaningful, relevant material

Figure 4.4
Web site illustrating the Content aspect. This site of the American Memory project contains accurate and reliable information.

Since Web sites do not always carry copyright dates, it is important to know when the site was last updated, especially if timeliness is important to the user. If students are researching an event in progress it will be important; however, if it's an historical topic, it's not critical. This date also indicates when the links were last checked. If a link is not working, the user will get a "404 Not Found" message. Web pages with consistent broken links indicate poor maintenance and are not good resources. Look to see if links are annotated, describing the contents of the linked page or, even better, include critical, evaluative annotations.

The Web site should provide information with depth and richness. Standard criteria that apply to print and other resources are also used to determine the quality of Web site content—accuracy, coverage, currency, and objectiveness. However, Web sites are not always analogous to print. The Web is a unique information source and so not all the ways we evaluate print will work on the Web.

Web sites should contain some original information, even if it just takes the form of photographs, videos, or charts to existing print material. Content-rich Web sites add to the existing body of knowledge on a topic. A reliable authority should be cited for all information (e.g. institutions, authors, publishers, etc.). When appropriate, different points of view or hypertext links to other sites representing alternative points of view should be included.

If multimedia applications are added, they should be relevant to the content. Some Webmasters add sound or video to their sites to attract users. These "extras," however, often do not add to content understanding, download slowly, and waste bandwidth. A good Web page will allow the user to choose if they want streaming audio/video or other additions. If the site contains primary source material, complete citation information should be included.

Design and Technical Features: Is the Web site well designed and does it operate efficiently?

Are the pages uncluttered with useful headings and subheadings?

Do the icons clearly represent what is intended?

Can you use a text-based browser?

Is the Web site accessible at most times of day?

Is the design consistent throughout the site?

Does it load in a reasonable amount of time?

Are there clear directions for locating and installing helper applications?

Can you print the contents of the page?

(See Figure 4.5.)

Provides a text-based browser

Appropriate children's theme

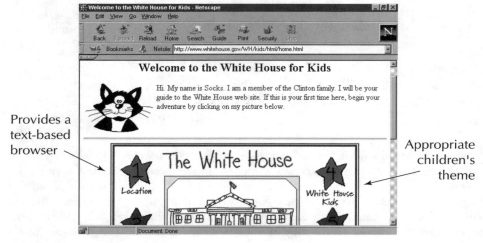

Figure 4.5
Web site illustrating Design and Technical aspects. This site is simple and uncluttered and the purpose is stated clearly.

A good Web page allows the user to perform desired tasks without frustration. The design is consistent throughout the site and has an uncluttered, organized screen with headings and sub-headings to help the user access the content. Icons such as arrows, mailboxes, and video players should be consistent, small, and true to what they represent. If helper applications are offered, there should be clear directions on how to download and use them. Webmasters cannot take it for granted that everyone understands and is familiar with the technology.

A well-designed Web site accommodates those without a fast modem or unlimited online time with a text-alternative. Text-based browsers only show "[IMAGE]" on their screen as a placeholder for a graphic image. Some pages have an enormous amount of graphics that considerably increase the time it takes to load a page. If a graphic is larger than 35K, the Web page designer should offer a smaller version, called a *thumbnail,* that allows users to select the larger graphic if they want to wait. If not, these sites become unwieldy and unusable. Printing the pages of a Web site is important for students doing research. Some sites that display the text in yellow or another light color cannot be read when printed.

Navigation: Can you move around the Web site easily?

Do external and internal links work?

Are the links clearly and accurately described?

Can you easily return to the home page from supporting pages?

Is there a searchable index, a site locator map, or help screens?

Are the navigation icons consistent throughout the site?

(See Figure 4.6.)

Text and background
aid in navigating

Hypertext and
links are clearly
marked
throughout
the site.

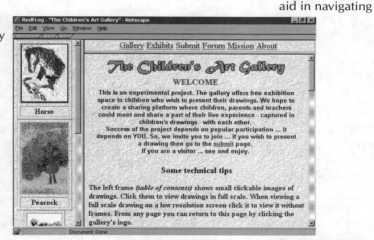

Some users are not familiar with frames.
Explanation is provided to help with navigation.

Figure 4.6
Web site illustrating the Navigation aspect. This site of The Children's Art Gallery allows the user to move around it easily.

A good Web page allows the user to move between screens and within screens, accessing information easily. Hypertext allows the user to jump from one place to another without moving in a straight or sequential fashion. To avoid confusion and the possibility of getting lost, navigation buttons back to the home page (first or top page of the site) should be carefully placed on each page. Some sites contain a searchable index or site locator map to help the user locate the information they want, which is more efficient than clicking and scrolling through pages of data. If they are well designed, they are a valuable addition to the page.

Curriculum Connections: Does the site support or enhance the curriculum?

Does the content correlate to the curriculum?

Does it support national content and performance standards?

Is the content unique and not available elsewhere?

Does the site offer instructional support materials?

Are the program objectives clearly stated?

(See Figures 4.7 and 4.8.)

Content is
unique.

Interactive
opportunities
for students.

Instructional
support is
provided.

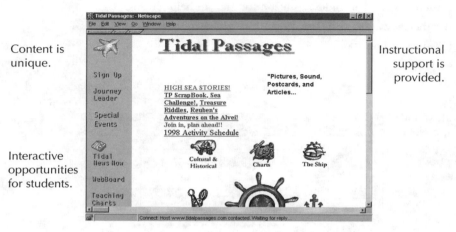

Figure 4.7

Web site illustrating Curriculum Connection aspect. The content of this Tidal Passages site relates to the curriculum.

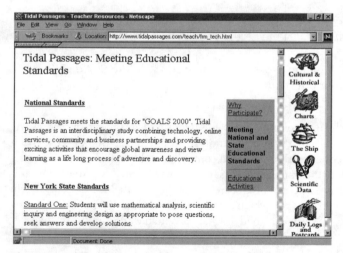

Figure 4.8

An extension of the Tidal Passages Web site, the content directly relates to the curriculum standards.

When we look at a Web site for educational use, it's important that we ask the same questions that we pose for any educational resource—does it relate to the curriculum? A good educational Web site will support the curriculum and engage students through the content and interactivity. An Internet Web site needs to match the curriculum, as does any other information resource. After potential sites are identified, group them according to curriculum area and consider how they support the curriculum. Ask questions such as: What content is covered? Do these Web sites contain information that is often requested by teachers and students? Can you identify specific instructional uses? Are there cross-curricular applications? Will it offer access to information unavailable in the school library media center? Will it support a frequently studied topic? Does it present the information in a unique way? It's very helpful when a site offers instructional support materials that contain student activities, (including off-line extensions of the program), management strategies, specific objectives, templates or examples of performance assessment strategies, and links to sites that support individual student needs according to ability levels, gender, and language.

Learning Environment: Is the site designed to take advantage of the unique capabilities of the Web? (information access, up-to-date information, publishing and communication)

Does the site provide ways for learners to share and display their work?

Does the site invite student input or collection data?

Does the Web site offer interactive opportunities?

Are student contributions and communications screened prior to posting?

Does the site offer access to information usually not available in school libraries?

Does the site offer access to current, up-to-date information?

Does the site encourage students to collaborate or communicate with other students or experts?

(See Figure 4.9.)

Students can share their work.

Encourages students to collaborate.

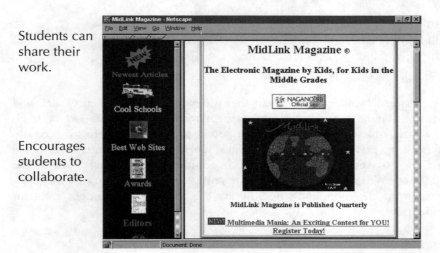

Figure 4.9
Web site illustrating the Learning Environment aspect. Student contributions at MidLink Magazine are reviewed by editors.

This section of the evaluation tool examines the educational connection. Questions focus on how the unique capabilities of the Web—information access, up-to-date information, publishing, and communication—are used to have an impact on student learning. Web sites should make effective use of currently available web features to increase the learning experience.

Some Web sites allow students to communicate with other students and experts around the country in meaningful dialogue and contribute to the collection of information on the site. Telecollaborative projects (such as Antarctica2) or a publishing site (such as MidLink) challenge students to get involved. An historical resource site, such as The New Deal, encourages students to add to the site's body of knowledge (refer to Chapter 6 for more information on these Web sites). Examine Web sites for incidences of student interactivity and then look at the methods used to assure quality. Are student contributions and communications screened prior to posting? (See Figure 4.10.)

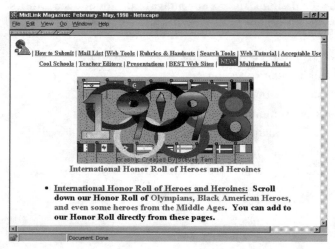

Figure 4.10
Web site illustrating a telecollaborative project. This special issue on the Olympians requests contributing participants.

If sites truly support student involvement, they will have ways for learners to share and display their work, online forms for student data input or collection, and support for development of a variety of student projects. Other good educational sites provide access to information that was previously never available in school library media centers, such as the Library of Congress' American Memory Page. In addition to the primary sources, the American Memory Web site provides The Learning Page to help educators use these primary sources in the classroom and school library. See http://memory.loc.gov/ammem/ndlpedu/index.html.

WEB SITE EVALUATION CHECKLIST

AUTHORITY: Who owns the Web site and why?

Is it clear who owns the Web site?

Is the purpose of the Web site to entertain, sell, educate, or persuade?

Is contact information for the Webmaster or author available?

CONTENT: Is the information accurate and reliable?

What is the author's expertise?

When was the information last updated?

Is any sort of bias evident?

Is the information well written and grammatically correct?

DESIGN AND NAVIGATION: Does the Web site function efficiently?

Is the graphic design appealing, with text that is easy to read?

Are the pages uncluttered, with useful headings and subheadings?

Is the design consistent throughout the Web site?

Do pages load in a reasonable amount of time?

CURRICULUM CONNECTIONS: Does the site enhance or support the curriculum?

Does the content correlate to the curriculum?

Is the content unique and not available elsewhere?

Does the site offer instructional materials?

LEARNING ENVIRONMENTS: Does the site incorporate the unique capabilities of the Web?

Does the site offer interactive opportunities?

Does the site provide ways for students or teachers to collaborate and/or share their work?

Does the site invite student input or collection data?

DEVELOP TARGETED EVALUATION FORMS

In working with students, a shorter, more targeted evaluation form that focuses on one or two sections of the longer form may be effective. The Evaluation form is very comprehensive, covering all aspects of Web site evaluation. It is helpful to break down the form into sections and teach students those parts that are meaningful to their immediate tasks.

Students being taught to identify and evaluate the content of cancer information sites will need a form targeted to that specific purpose—Authority and Content (see sample in box).

A form targeted to the development of Web sites, including Navigation and Design and Technical Features, would be helpful to a group of students learning about web page design. The complete form is available on the ICONnect Web site at http://www.ala.org/ ICONN.Download it, bring it into a word processing or desk top publishing program, and cut and paste the sections to meet the instructional needs of your students.

STUDENT WEB SITE EVALUATION CHECKLIST

Who owns the Web site?

Is it affiliated with an organization or institution or does an
    individual own the site?

_____

What is the purpose of the Web site?

Is it to entertain, persuade, educate, or sell?
Explain:_____

Who is the author of the information?

What is the author's expertise on the subject? Is the author's
    education, position or education provided? Is contact
    information for the author available?

_____

How recent is the information?

When was the Web site last updated?

_____

Is the information well written and grammatically correct?

_____

Does the site contain links to other sites that reflect a bias?

_____

Is the information meaningful and useful for your research?
Explain:_____

DEVELOP AGE-SPECIFIC EVALUATION FORMS

It's important for students, even at a very young age, to become information literate. Elementary age students can be introduced to web evaluation skills thorough the curriculum as they locate and evaluate information for their own information needs or school projects. Various sites on the Web have included specialized evaluation forms for elementary, middle, and secondary students. Kathy Schrock's Educator's Page at http:// www.capecod.net/schrockguide/eval.htm provides tools targeted to three age groups—elementary, middle, and high school students. Kathy also includes a lesson plan on teaching

Web evaluation to elementary students. When you visit this site to look at the evaluation forms, be sure to explore the entire site and bookmark it. It's one of the best educational sites on the Web. Kathy Schrock is a library media specialist who works at a Cape Cod, Massachusetts, high school as the technology director. She offers a constant supply of relevant educational Web sites and other value-added content.

When developing evaluation questions for younger students, keep it simple. Confine it to one page with two sections at the most. Concentrate on questions that can be answered with yes or no, and include a summary question asking if the student would recommend the site to a classmate and why. Be sure to include questions regarding safety, inquiring if the site asks for personal information. Young children need to become aware of safety issues when navigating the Web.

ADVANCED STRATEGY

Develop a student evaluation project in your school. Visit the K.I.D.S. Report (Kids Identifying and Discovering Sites), a publication produced by K–12 students as a resource to other K–12 students. This ongoing, cooperative effort of two classrooms in the Madison, Wisconsin, Madison Metropolitan School District and two classrooms in the Boulder, Colorado, Boulder Valley School District can be used as a model. Selection criteria are included as information to all readers of the K.I.D.S. Report for consideration by other students who may want to use similar criteria when identifying and selecting Internet sites for their own Web pages. Publication of the K.I.D.S. Report is biweekly throughout the 1997-98 school year. The Report focuses on a theme, such as Math Fun, the Planets, Native Americans, Irresistible Resources, and Cool Connections. Past publications are archived on the site.

TIP

Have students develop their own evaluation form to use in your school. Brainstorm questions that are important to them, develop the form, test it out, and continue to refine it. Post it on the library home page for other students to comment on and use.

COMPARE WEB SITES TO TEACH EVALUATION

When teaching students to evaluate Web sites, it's important to get them actively involved in analyzing the features rather than focusing on collecting information for their report. It's helpful for students when first learning how to evaluate a Web site to look at sites that illustrate the concepts being taught. In preparation for the lesson, decide on the evaluation criteria that you want the students to become proficient in and cut and paste the section of the evaluation form with the appropriate questions. Identify a few Web sites that distinctly meet that criteria and a few that clearly don't. Briefly explain the evaluation criteria, assign the Web sites to the student teams/pairs and instruct them fill out a modified evaluation form for each of the web sites being examined. Bring the class back together and ask each team to explain their findings. As an example, when teaching the concepts of Authority/Credibility and Content, the following Web sites usually work effectively.

TIP
Open two screens in Windows to place Web sites side by side while demonstrating evaluation of Web sites. Teach students how to do the same.

Compare These Sites

Court TV at http://www.courttv.com with the Legal Information Institute's Hermes Supreme Court page at http://supct.law.cornell.edu/supct.

The White House Page at http://www.whitehouse.gov with the "alternate" White House at http//: www.whitehouse.net.

OncoLink at http://oncolink.upenn.edu/ with the American Smokers Alliance http://www.smokers.org.

CONDUCT A WEB EVALUATION WORKSHOP

Don't expect educators to intuitively know how to evaluate Web sites. It takes practice and a familiarity with the Internet. Invite teachers and administrators to a short workshop on evaluating the World Wide Web. It will be helpful to demonstrate how to evaluate a Web site, using a computer with a large display monitor. Many teachers have limited experience with the Internet and little or no experience with evaluating a Web site. Design the workshop to have time for hands-on exploration, if possible. Discuss the unique features of the Web that make it such a powerful medium to use in education, explaining the various types of Web pages, and showing examples of each. Have teachers work collaboratively in pairs or small groups. Distribute evaluation forms along with specific Web sites to explore and evaluate during the second part of the workshop. Be sure to include quality sites and weak sites, as well as different types of sites. Bring the groups together at the end of the session to discuss the Web sites, how they rated them, and why.

TIP
Distribute the results of the Evaluation Workshop to the faculty in a listing of annotated sites. Give credit to the participating faculty and include the date and place of the next evaluation workshop.

NETWORK WITH COLLEAGUES

Join listservs to discuss how Web sites are being used in different curriculum areas. ICON-CURR, run by AASL and facilitated by Debbie Abilock from the Nueva School in California, has an ongoing discussion focusing on the theory and application of learning, Web evaluation, and curriculum integration. LM_Net allows easy and timely sharing of personal experience with using various Web sites. Both positive and negative comments are helpful. Web4Lib is for librarians using the Web.

IDENTIFY AWARD WEB SITES/REVIEW GUIDES

It's helpful to look at Web sites that conduct ongoing, continuous identification and rating of other Web sites. These sites can save time sifting through large amounts of information, but remember, they do not eliminate the need for evaluation. Be sure to look at their evaluation criteria. It is usually contained on the Web page and can be printed out for closer scrutiny. Don't trust all Award Sites. Many consider a site's entertainment or coolness value in their evaluation and do not attempt to rate content accuracy. Carefully examine them and choose ones that you feel are reliable. When you evaluate an award site, be sure to check who sponsored the award, who the judges were, what their qualifications were, and what the specific evaluation criteria were. There are some sites, such as the Web 100 at http://www.Web 100.com that focus on popularity rather than standard criteria.

In the box is a brief list of valuable award sites. Visit these sites, look at the criteria, and decide which sites are most likely to keep you informed.

AWARD SITES

Blue Web'N - Education Learning Applications
    http://www.kn.pacbell.com/wired/bluewebn

Ed's Oasis
    http://www.EdsOasis.org/Treasure/Treasure.html

Eisenhower National Clearinghouse for Mathematics and Science's Digital Dozen
    http://www.enc.org/classroom/index.htm

Global Information Infrastructure (GII) Award
    http://www.gii-awards.com/

Point Communications Top 5% Sites
    http://point.lycos.com/categories/index.html

Software Publishers Association Codie Awards
    http://www.spa.org

Webbie Awards
    http://www.marketcentral.com/Webbies/

INVOLVE TEACHERS WITH EVALUATION

It is important to involve teachers in the process of evaluating Web sites, not only for their input as content and curriculum specialists, but also to acquaint them with what is available. Approach them individually and consider requesting time at faculty and department meetings to share information on Web sites you have identified. Take advantage of teacher's help in rating sites and identifying curriculum tie-ins. Explain how you selected these sites and solicit their help to targeting more sites.

To begin this process, go to the ICONnect Web site at http://www.ala.org/ICONN Curriculum Connections section. Choose the subject specific sections, then click on any one of the curriculum areas. Print out the list of evaluated, annotated sites for the specific curriculum. Photocopy the pages and put one in each teacher's mailbox. Include a note from you, suggesting they take a look at these sites and mentioning how one or two of them would support their curriculum. Suggest they stop in the library to talk to you about how it.

ADVANCED STRATEGY
Review Web sites on the National School Network Web site at http://nsn.bbn.com/webeval/backup_site_feedback.html. Educators are provided the opportunity to review educationally useful Web sites, search the archive for sites others have reviewed, or join a discussion of the Web sites and their educational uses by entering your review. Sites requesting educator's evaluation and feedback are listed on the site.

ENCOURAGE STUDENTS TO EVALUATE SITES FOR THE VIRTUAL LIBRARY PAGE

It is not enough for school library media specialists (or only faculty) to judge a Web site. Students should be encouraged to become knowledgeable consumers of electronic information. What better way than to be involved in evaluating Web sites for the school community? Include a program on your Virtual Library Page for students to comment on Web sites that are on the virtual library page and new ones that they want to recommend. Community School Network at http://www.csnet.net offers web-based tools for educators to use to encourage students to become actively involved. The Living Page allows users to contribute URLs with comments directly on the Virtual Library Page to share with the school community.

For those students and faculty who are not regular Internet navigators, have print forms available in the school library media center for them to recommend Web sites for the Virtual Library Page. They will be more likely to use the Virtual Library Page once they have contributed to its content. To encourage students and faculty to critically evaluate the site before recommending it, include a few evaluation questions and space for suggested curriculum tie-ins in the form.

Chapter 5

Integrating the Internet into the Curriculum

With the Internet comes the potential of bringing immediacy, individualization, and creative approaches to the school curriculum. To employ the full potential of the Web in the teaching and learning process, it's important to look at the unique features of the medium. Each technology has strengths that it brings to the learning environment. Computer software offered the user feedback for the first time. CD-ROMs provided the added benefit of multimedia elements, sound, graphics, and video on one disc. Now the Internet presents the highest degree of interactivity by building on those previous technologies. It offers communication (the ability to communicate with learners around the world), contribution (the opportunity to publish and contribute original work), access to unique and timely information, the ability to locate primary source material and other information never before available, and interactivity (the opportunity to participate in active learning environments).

The Internet offers access to information that was never available before in a school library. Foreign language students read up-to-date newspapers from countries all over the world, choosing from among 15 to 20 native-language newspapers from just one country. Health students researching cancer causes and prevention access the latest statistics and research from the American Cancer Society and the National Institute for Health Web pages. Social studies students locate up-to-date information on environmental legislation, e-mail their senators and representatives, discuss issues, and have their opinions heard on specialized listservs. Science students work side-by-side with scientists in Antarctica and the South Pacific through telecollaborative projects, sharing data collection and analysis. Economics students studying the stock market retrieve up-to-the-minute stock quotes, late breaking company news, and in-depth analysis that two years ago would have bestowed the competitive edge upon an investor. Now it's available to everyone on the Web.

Technology can create experiences for students to become active learners by shifting the focus from ingesting information to constructing understanding. Use the Internet to change students from passive recipients of information to active information-literate producers. The Internet's power is based on its interactive capabilities; it offers students the chance to collaborate and contribute to the information base. Students engage in in-depth collaborative projects that investigate the real world. That's what it's all about—kids "doing" the thinking, and kids "doing" the technology. Computer technology can spur the design for new learning environments by incorporating inquiry-based learning, authentic learning tasks, interdisciplinary curricula, new forms of assessment, and new roles for teachers and librarians. Technology can be a catalyst to educational reform. It can be used to change or restructure the teaching/learning environment.

FOCUS ON STUDENT LEARNING

Integrating Internet resources into the curriculum is not simple, nor is there one single "right" way to do it. Technology can be used in numerous situations, processes, and curricula.

It should be viewed as a tool to enhance learning and possibly to restructure the learning environment, but not as the solution to all problems in education. The power of technology lies in its ability to create more effective learning experiences, thereby increasing students' active learning. Don't be fooled by the glitzy lure of technology; the mere introduction of computer hardware and software to the library or classroom is not enough. Focus on the student learning. You are wasting time and money if the technology you offer doesn't have an impact on students by motivating them and involving them in their own learning and channeling them into becoming active learners. They need to be intellectually active—comparing, contrasting, organizing, analyzing, and constructing knowledge.

Unfortunately, technology is being used all too often in the same old, narrow way—to identify and deliver information without any analysis. Now obtaining information is easier than ever before—just point and click. Kids will aimlessly wander around the Internet without a strategy or an understanding of what they are looking for. Students need to learn how to locate information effectively through an in-depth understanding of search engines, Boolean searching, wildcards, and other search strategies. They need to evaluate information by critically examining the authority and the content of the Web site.

The strategies and resources in the next two chapters are suggestions to help you incorporate the Internet into your curriculum. It doesn't matter whether you start with an existing curriculum unit, a favorite Web site, a WebQuest, or a telecollaborative project, as long as you focus on using technology to make students active learners. Continually ask yourself: How is this use of technology different? How is this affecting student learning? These strategies and Web resources can help you get a jumpstart. The best ones are those that evolve or are discovered naturally from collaborative curriculum development between the school librarian and teachers.

STRATEGY 1—USE TECHNOLOGY TO TEACH INFORMATION LITERACY SKILLS

Incorporating information literacy skills into the curriculum along with Internet resources is an effective use of the Internet and serves multiple purposes. It broadens the scope of the current curriculum unit, gives kids an opportunity to learn about Web resources, and helps them hone their information literacy skills. Information literacy—the ability to locate, organize, evaluate, and use information—is an essential requirement for the twenty-first century. All curriculum units, projects, and lesson plans should incorporate these processes to allow students to practice and hone their skills. Information literacy is not the outcome of one curriculum unit, but rather the cumulative experience for a range of subjects and learning experiences, all of which create the information literate person.

The American Association of School Librarians (AASL) and Association of Educational Communications and Technology (AECT) developed student information literacy standards. Point your browser to http://www.ala.org/aasl and download a copy of the Information Literacy Standards. The first three of the nine standards define the information literate student.

A student who is information literate:

Standard 1. Accesses information efficiently and effectively, as described by the following indicators:
1. recognizes the need for information
2. recognizes that accurate and comprehensive information is the basis for intelligent decision making

3. formulates questions based on information needs

4. identifies a variety of potential sources of information

5. develops and uses successful strategies for locating information

Standard 2. Evaluates information critically and competently, as described by the following indicators:

1. determines accuracy, relevance, and comprehensiveness

2. distinguishes among fact, point of view, and opinion

3. identifies inaccurate and misleading information

4. selects information appropriate to the problem or question at hand

Standard 3. Uses information effectively and creatively, as described by the following indicators:

1. organizes information for practical application

2. integrates new information into one's own knowledge

3. applies information in critical thinking and problem solving

4. produces and communicates information and ideas in appropriate formats

(See Figure 5.1.)

Figure 5.1
Information Literacy Standards for Student Learning.

For students to be information literate, they must know how to use Internet applications and functions effectively. By incorporating these applications into the curriculum you are both creating an active learning environment and giving students an opportunity to learn how to be information literate. These applications include e-mail, listservs, Moos, IRC, CU-SeeMe, web navigation, search engines and directories, gopher, FTP, HTML and authoring programs, and downloading and uploading files. These Internet applications directly support the three information skills of accessing, organizing, and evaluating information.

MOO Stands for "Multi-user domain, Object-Oriented." It's a social environment in a text-based virtual reality where people gather to chat with friends, meet new people, and help build the MOO. Users are called "players" or "characters" and can connect from anywhere in the world and communicate with others in real time. To experience a MOO, go to http://miamimoo.moo. mcs.muohio.edu.

IRC Stands for "Internet Relay Chat." This is a live-talk infrastructure on the Internet that enables multiple users to communicate in real time. Logon to http://www.irchelp.org for more information.

CU-SeeMe A free videoconferencing program available to anyone with a Windows or Macintosh computer and a connection to the Internet. It allows geographically separate students and educators to see and hear each other, across the world or across the classroom, with only a small, relatively inexpensive camera plugged into the personal computer.

ICONnect

Learn about new technologies on the Web. Sign up for a free online course, Trends in Interactivity, on the ICONnect Web site. Learn about Plug-ins, three-dimensional images, MOOs, Virtual Reality, Java, and more. Maybe even stay one step ahead of your students!

TIP

For an in-depth discussion on incorporating Internet functions into the curriculum with information searching skills, see Mike Eisenberg and Doug Johnson's article, Computer Skills for Information Problem Solving: Learning and Teaching Technology in Context at http://ericir. syr.edu/ithome/digests/computerskills.html.

Access and Organize Information

Teach students how to navigate the Web using Web browsers, such as Netscape Communicator or Internet Explorer. Demonstrate how to bookmark sites they need to save and organize the sites in folders according to assignments, curriculum areas, or other logical topics. Students need to know how to download and save their bookmark files to use on their home computers. They also need to know how to send a web page to themselves via the Web.

Incorporate opportunities within the curriculum for students to e-mail teachers and classmates. They will soon realize how effective and efficient e-mail is when they can quickly and easily contact their teachers and classmates to discuss homework assignments, collaborative projects, and presentations. Require students to locate and collect information using search engines and directories. Often students think they have mastered the art of locating information on the Web because they are frequent users (mostly in chat rooms and games), but often they have not learned the necessary strategies for effective use of Web search engines. Young children in elementary school can be taught to access appropriate information on virtual library pages and school pages using point-and-click skills, and they can learn functions such as Print and Bookmark. Chapter 3 addresses the basics of the popular search engines and provides practical strategies and tips for saving bookmarks.

When students locate information, they need to be able to download, decompress, and open documents from Web sites on the Internet, whether the documents are in text, numerical, or graphic files. When developing units and scouting out resources to recommend to students, be sure to include numerical information such as data from the U.S. Census, photographs, paintings or images from sites such as the Library of Congress or NASA, and sound clips from sites such as the National Public Radio.

ICONnect
Learn how to teach students to be information literate in the twenty-first century. Sign up to take the free online course, Information Literacy and the Internet, on the ICONnect Web site. Learn the skills you need to integrate technology and information literacy into the curriculum.

Increase student collaboration through communication tools such as e-mail, listservs, chat, newsgroups, and electronic conferencing. Students can use these tools to communicate with experts internationally, as well as with students in neighboring school districts. Simple collaborative activities, such as language arts students editing each other's essays, can be a valuable telecollaborative project. Students using e-mail can share scientific data, short stories, journals, and poetry. They can discuss books and environmental concerns and compare local culture, food, or real estate prices. Help students understand Internet netiquette when communicating with experts and peers. Encourage students to organize information through the design and development of Web sites using hypertext markup language (HTML) or Web site authoring software programs such as Microsoft's Front Page or Adobe Pagemill.

Evaluate Information

Guide students in the evaluation of Web sites. Many students think that if the information is on the Internet or a computer, it must be true. This naiveté exists among novice Internet-using teachers too. Stress that every Web site must be examined with scrutiny and compared to print and other sources. Chapter 4 explains, in depth, the evaluation process and the tools and strategies needed to actively involve teachers and students.

Teach students to document electronic resources. As they start to navigate the Internet they will need to learn how to document the sources accurately. Incorporate mini-lessons to teach these skills and be sure to allow time to practice. For suggestions of Web sites to help you teach documentation, consider the following. The Sarah Byrd Askew Library Web site has a "Guide for Citing Electronic Resources" at http://www.wilpaterson.edu/wpcpages/library/citing.htm and the "Bibliography Styles Handbook" can be found at http://www.english.uiuc.edu/cws/wworkshop/bibliostyles.htm.

ICONnect
Find out what other school librarians are doing that works! Look at successful Internet-integrated curriculum projects on the ICONnect Web site. Connect to the Curriculum Connections section to look at curriculum units, or "best practices," that effectively incorporate information literacy and technology. View the Mini-Grants section to look at recent winners' curriculum projects.

TIP
Check out these information skills models: *Information Problem Solving* by Mike Eisenberg and Robert E. Berkowitz. (1990, Ablex Publishing Corporation, Norwood, N.J. http://ericir.syr.edu/bigb/bigsix.html); *Pathways to Knowledge,* by Marjorie Pappas and Anne Teppe. (1997, Follett Software Company, McHenry, Illinois, http://www.pathwaysmodel.com); and *Brainstorms and Blueprints* Barbara K. Striping and Judy M. Pitts. (1988, Libraries Unlimited, Englewood, Colo.).

STRATEGY 2—GO ON A WEBQUEST

In 1995, Bernie Dodge, a professor of educational technology at San Diego State University, developed WebQuests for his university classes and promptly posted a three-page explanation of this new Internet-based activity on the Web. Word spread quickly on the Web; teachers, school media specialists, and other university professors studied this unique approach to using the Internet and developed auxiliary materials to support the teaching of WebQuests. Since then, K–12 educators have used his innovative idea to successfully integrate Internet resources into their curriculum.

WebQuest is an inquiry-oriented activity in which some or all of the information that learners interact with comes from resources on the Internet and conceptually incorporate Marzano's Dimension of Thinking Model. WebQuests can be used with any subject and at any grade level. They are designed to make the best use of a learner's time.

A WebQuest has six components:

1. an introduction that sets the stage and provides some background information
2. a task that is doable and interesting
3. a set of information resources needed to complete the task
4. a description of the process the learners should go through in accomplishing the task
5. guidance on how to organize the information
6. a conclusion that brings closure to the quest, reminding the learners about what they have learned

WebQuest Levels

There are two levels of WebQuests: short term and long term. The short-term WebQuest's instructional goal is knowledge acquisition and integration from the Web, as well as from in-school resources. Students ultimately create web pages. At the end of a short-term WebQuest, the learner will have grappled with a significant amount of new information and made sense of it. It is completed in one to three class periods. The long-term WebQuest challenges students to extend and refine the information and demonstrate their under-standing of the material by creating something that others can respond to, online or off-line. The emphasis is on the thinking and information skills and will take between one week and a month to complete. Longer term WebQuest activities might require students to compare, classify, induce, deduce, analyze errors, construct support, abstract, or analyze perspectives according to Marzano's Dimensions of Thinking.

Learn about WebQuests

The best way to learn about WebQuests is to look at a few examples. Start at the WebQuest home page at http://edweb.sdsu.edu/webquest/webquest.html. From there you can read Bernie Dodge's concept paper explaining the concepts behind WebQuest and look at train-ing materials, such as a slide show by Kathy Schrock, and lesson templates. A section called "Building Blocks" helps educators develop their own WebQuests, and there is an actual WebQuest on WebQuests! Courses that teach about WebQuests at San Diego State University and San Francisco State University and examples of WebQuests are also available. A matrix of examples by grade level and subject is listed as well as WebQuests developed by individuals and classes from Bridgewater State University, New Mexico State University, and Indiana University. As you look through the WebQuest examples, note that most are likely to be group activities. The learners often have a role to play and the WebQuests are often interdisciplinary. (See Figure 5.2.)

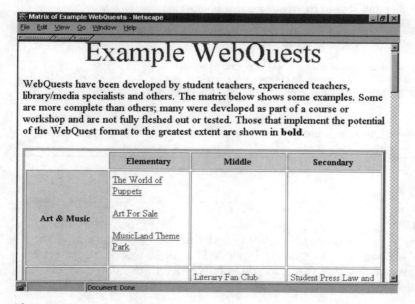

Figure 5.2
Find example WebQuests at this site. WebQuests help integrate the Internet into a curriculum.

WEBQUESTS TO EXPLORE

Hello Dolly: A WebQuest on Cloning

http://204.102.137.135/PUSDRBHS/science/clone/dolly.htm

Searching for China by Tom March

http://www.kn.pacbell.com/wired/China/ChinaQuest.html

The AmericanDream…Through the Decades by Leni Donlan and Kathleen Ferenz

http:\\www.town.put.kiz.ca.us/Collaborations/amproject/student.html

The Real Scoop on Tobacco

http://www.itdc.sbcss.k12.ca.us/curriculum/tobacco.html

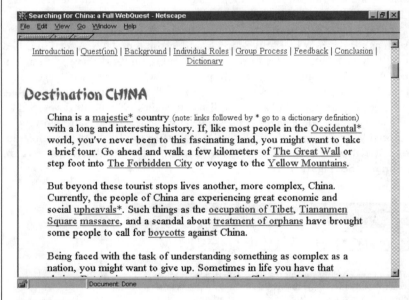

Figure 5.3
This sample WebQuest is Searching for China. Follow the links to learn more.

TIP
Before you develop a WebQuest for your students, take the WebQuest on a WebQuest developed by Bernie Dodge. Suggest to a few teachers that they join you at http://edweb.sdsu.edu/webquest/webquest.html.

ICONnect

Discuss important issues, theory, and strategies to integrate the Internet into the curriculum with your colleagues. Point your browser to the ICONnect Web site and click on Curriculum Connections. If you are an AASL member, join the ICONN CURR listserv. If not, go http://www.ala.org/AASL and join. Don't miss out on this important discussion.

STRATEGY 3—TEACH STUDENTS TO USE COMPUTER APPLICATIONS

As you integrate the Internet into the curriculum, you will automatically start to use other computer applications, such as word processing, spreadsheets, databases, presentation and authoring programs, and graphic organizers. Language Arts students can use word processing skills to write articles for MidLink magazine at http://longwood.cs.ucf.edu/~MidLink/. Science students will use spreadsheets to collect, organize, and analyze their weather data before they post it on the Kids as Global Scientists Web site at http://onesky.engin.umich.edu. kgs98/index.980116.html. Social Studies students can use databases to organize their data and print out customized reports to send via e-mail to collaborating students in projects such as Youth for Social Action at http://www.mightymedia.com/youth/. Students designing web pages will find graphic organizers very helpful.

Curriculum can be developed or existing curriculum updated to ensure that students work regularly with relevant information resources. Look carefully at lesson plans and choose ones that will benefit from the integration of a technology such as the Internet. Technology both requires and supports active learning, so lesson plans that incorporate higher order level thinking and information processing skills will work best with technology integration. To incorporate technology such as the Internet, you must update traditional lesson plans with learning activities that incorporate information and critical thinking skills.

As you look at your favorite lesson plans, think to yourself, What are the students doing? If the activities in the lesson plan leave the students to consume the information passively while the teacher lectures or supplies the relevant content through textbooks and photocopied sheets, it needs to be updated. Traditional resources are fine, but only when used with electronic resources that encourage active learning. Design activities that have students locate, evaluate, and present information using the functions and resources of the Internet.

The chart in Figure 5.4 will help you to focus on student learning. Computer applications are organized around student activities: collecting, organizing, using, and presenting information. As you develop the curriculum, consider how you can incorporate these computer applications into your lessons. Rather than note cards, teach students to use a database or word processing when writing and e-mail to collaborate with experts and to hand in assignments.

TECHNOLOGY/CURRICULUM INTEGRATION

Use technology as a tool to empower students to be actively involved in their learning through the information skills process and computer application programs

What Is the Learner Doing?	Types of Tools	Technology Applications
Locating	Information Access Tool	Online Catalog
Searching		CD-ROM ⟨ networked reference titles / circulating multimedia titles
		Internet/ ⟨ information sources / interactive/telecollaborative sites
		Web sites fee-based full-text information
Collaborating	Communication/ Collaboration Tool	e-mail Internet listservs groupware chat video conference visual tools
Organizing	Organization Tool	databases spreadsheets Web pages statistical software graphic organizers
Producing	Writing/Authoring Tool	word processing multimedia authoring desktop publishing
Sharing	Visual Display Tool	presentation programs graphic design

Figure 5.4
Technology/Curriculum Integration Chart.

STRATEGY 4—JOIN A TELECOLLABORATIVE PROJECT

Project Based Learning on the Internet

Telecollaborative project work has its beginning in Project Based Learning, which is not new to education. John Dewey and his colleagues did the most well-known work in the 1920s. Since then educators and reformers have used projects to change the learning experience, increase student's ownership and motivation, and provide opportunities to apply skills. With the advent of technology, project work takes on an added dimension.

A project is an in-depth investigation of a topic worth learning about. It consists of an individual or group engaging in a long-term activity that results in either new knowledge and/or new artifacts. The goal is to find out more about the topic rather than to seek right answers. Projects are primarily used to motivate students and create more effective learning experiences. For a more detailed discussion of the Project Approach go to http://ericps. crc.uiuc.edu/eece/pubs/digests/1994/lk-pro94.html to read "The Project Approach" by Lillian Katz.

There are many advantages in combining project work with the power of technology to develop telecollaborative activities. Using technology in project-based work makes the environment more authentic to students. The computer provides data and information that students never before had access to; it expands interaction and collaboration with others via e-mail, listservs, bulletin boards, etc., and emulates tools experts use to produce artifacts. The World Wide Web enhances project-based learning by offering students a unique opportunity to share (publish) their learning projects with millions of others and to build ongoing dialog among the project authors, experts, and learners. It's a great presentation medium, and it has multiple communication tools for collaboration and unlimited resources for research. The unique features of the Web combined with the traditional and effective teaching strategy of project-based learning creates a powerful learning environment.

Project work does not constitute the whole curriculum, but it is used instead to complement the more formal parts of the curriculum. It should not be considered an "add on" either, since it provides a context for applying concepts and skills. It's difficult to neatly categorize telecollaborative projects. Most projects fit the general description and have similar goals (as stated in the preceding paragraph), but the structure is based on the topic being explored, individual teaching styles, classroom resources, and pedagogical goals being followed in the design.

ADVANCED STRATEGY

Al Rogers outlines important pedagogical, political, social, cultural, and economic reasons why schools should consider telecommunications technologies as a learning tool. Read his article at http://www. gsn.org/teach/articles/gutenberg.html. In particular, examine the reasons why students' learning changes when they participate/telecollaborate in a global village, and for teacher analysis of student involvement and achievement.

Judi Harris at the University of Texas at Austin has developed a Web site with both E-Mail-Based Telecollaborative Activities (http://lrs.ed.uiuc.edu/Activity-Structures /Harris-

Activity-Structures.html) and Web-Based Telecollaborative Activities (http://lrs.ed. uiuc.edu/Activity-Structures/web-activity-structures.html). Read her articles online or print them out for a better understanding of the varied types of telecollaborative activity students and teachers are currently involved in. The articles explain each type of activity structures with specific examples in all different curriculum areas. An overview of all of the collections can be found at http://lrs.ed.uiuc.edu/Activity-Structures/.

Three major activity structures are outlined with examples:

1. Interpersonal exchanges—http://www.ed.uiuc.edu/Mining/March95-TCT.html

   Keypals pen-pal exchanges between individuals or groups

   Global Classrooms two or more classrooms studying a common topic together

   Electronic "Appearances" short-term guest experts

   Electronic Mentoring long-term relationship between expert and student or class

   Question and Answer Services experts answering questions

   Impersonations role-playing

2. Information collection—http://www.ed.uiuc.edu/Mining/April95-TCT.html

   Information Exchanges collecting and exchanging thematically related information

   Database Creations organizing collected information into databases that can be used for study

   Electronic Publishing publishing a common document

   "Telefieldtrips" sharing observations from local and long distance travel

   Pooled Data Analysis analysis of data collected at multiple sites

3. Problem solving projects—http://www.ed.uiuc.edu/Mining/May95-TCT.html

   Information Searches looking for answers to staged problems

   Electronic Process Writing engaging in reflection and critical practice

   Parallel Problem Solving sharing solutions and results of activities

   Sequential Creations building a common text or image

   Virtual Gatherings coming together in cyberspace

   Simulations role-playing events

   Social Action Projects creating change in the world outside the classroom

ADVANCED STRATEGY

Yvonne Marie Andres addresses the issue of collaborating in her article "Collaboration in the Classroom and Over the Internet." She argues that the Internet is one of the most exciting and effective ways to teach students how to both communicate and collaborate by connecting teams of students with other classrooms around the world. Logon to http://www.gsn.org/teach/articles/collaboration.html. Andres outlines steps to take to be better prepared before, during, and after collaboration.

Formal Telecollaborative Projects

There are several formal telecollaborative projects available online to educators. These are sponsored by educational networks and organizations committed to education and are very often represented by a Web site. By using a formal model of project-based learning, the project template and much of the groundwork is done for you. Consequently, you participate through their already established telecommunications, guidelines, and networked activities. Many projects offer extensive lesson plans and/or curriculum guides that support the learning objectives for the project. Several outstanding models exist and are annotated here. Many of the cited projects are interdisciplinary in nature.

Visit each site and explore the structure, pedagogical goals, curricular focus, interdisciplinary activities, and timeframes of past and present online projects. Be sure and check if there is a fee for participation. Significant links within each site are noted to indicate telecollaborative highlights. Sites are listed alphabetically.

ICONnect
Learn more about telecollaborative projects. Sign up for a free online course at the ICONnect Web site, Telecollaborative Activities on the Internet. Learn how to find out about new projects, develop your own project, and more.

Adventure Online

http://www.adventureonline.com

Adventure Online, sponsored by Event Media, is an interactive project that will take your students on virtual journeys that connect to science and social studies curricula. Past adventures include Running the Nile, Eco-Adventures on McKinley, Project Central America, and the International Greenland Expedition. On this last journey, two arctic sea persons, one from the United States and one from Greenland, traveled the arctic by dog team and kayak to make the first circumnavigation of the world's largest island, Greenland. Adventures offered daily lessons, classroom activities, photos and templates for multi-media presentations, journal updates, and more. Participants linked to Newsstands and Lessons and viewed the "Expedition News" archives or subscribed to receive a monthly review of expeditions, research projects, and adventures. Logon to read about Project Magellan and the Arctic Challenge.

*CoVis—Learning Through Collaborative Visualization

http://www.covis.nwu.edu

CoVis, the Learning Through Collaborative Visualization Project at Northwestern University, focusing on K–12 science education, "provides students with a range of collaboration and communication tools" and projects that include desktop video conferencing; shared software environments for remote, real-time collaboration; scientific visualization software; a multimedia scientist's "notebook"; and access to Internet resources. Choose the Geosciences WebServer link to access Activities,

Resources, the Teacher Lounge, Student Lounge, CoVis Information, and Community News. Link to Activities to find a variety of science-based telecollaborative Internet projects.

The Global Schoolhouse (GSH)

http://www.gsh.org/

Sponsored by Microsoft and the Global SchoolNet Foundation, The Global Schoolhouse is an outstanding resource that provides the Projects Registry Database, "a comprehensive source for Internet-based classroom projects." Choose the Connected Classroom link to view current and past projects or to register your own. Use the Project Registry, searchable by keyword, title, subject, organization, grade level, and the month the project begins, to link to the project site of your choice. This site makes the sometimes overwhelming task of finding a customized online project manageable, efficient, and fun! (See Figure 5.5.)

Figure 5.5
The Global Schoolhouse is an excellent resource for Internet-based classroom projects.

Global SchoolNet Foundation (GSN)

http://www.gsn.org

The Global SchoolNet Foundation, a nonprofit organization founded by teachers, provides access to high-technology online projects and curricular support for educators. The Projects Registry allows you the convenience of viewing projects from many sponsors (GSH, I*EARN, NASA, and others) by the month that they are available so that you can plan ahead. Link to the Global SchoolNet Projects which require only one dedicated Internet line or e-mail access only, such as "Scientists on Tap" or the "Mad Scientist Network." Or travel the world with Travel Buddies at Oz via the Teachernet link.

ICONnect
Point your browser to the ICONnect Web site at http://www.ala. org/ICONN and click on Online Courses. Sign up for the online course on telecollaborative projects to learn how to find out about new projects, how to decide which one is best for you, how to develop your own telecollaborative project, and more.

I*EARN

http://www.igc.apc.org/iearn/

I*EARN, the International Education and Resource Network, "enables young people to undertake projects designed to make a meaningful contribution to the health and welfare of the planet and its people." It offers the education community structured projects in social studies, science, mathematics, the arts, literature, and interdisciplinary areas. Link to I*EARN Projects and explore interactive projects by subject area. Check out The Holocaust/Genocide Project, under Social Studies, which allows students to explore the historical, political, and human actions and responses in relation to the Holocaust, genocide, and current bias and hate crimes. I*EARN also sponsors Learning Circles by which telecollaborative partnerships among schools from around the world are established. Many of the projects and links are available in both English and Spanish.

The JASON Project

http://www.jasonproject.org/

The JASON Project, founded by Dr. Robert D. Ballard after his discovery of the RMS Titanic and sponsored by The National Geographic Society, brings students on two-week "electronic field trips" broadcast in real-time via telecommunications. Link to Expedition and Journey to the Center of the Earth with the JASON VIII project, through which teachers and students travel to Iceland and Yellowstone National Park with the JASON Expedition. Detailed curriculum guides are available to guide the teacher through the expedition with telecollaborative lessons. Use the Teachers' Guide for broadcast dates, curriculum tips, online connection information, and more! Perform a keyword or subject search of all JASON projects for a topic of your interest. The JASON Project also offers a Bulletin Board where news, project updates, and teacher and student discussion groups are posted. (See Figure 5.6.)

Figure 5.6
The JASON Project is another great place to have students interact with
the Internet. Here students are able to take virtual field trips.

NASA K–12 Internet Initiative: Quest

http://quest.arc.nasa.gov/

This comprehensive site, sponsored by NASA, brings authentic scientific and engineering experiments and pursuits "out of the box and ready to go to classrooms
around the world." Use the Online Interactive Projects link to access NASA-sponsored
online interactive projects which features current projects, upcoming projects,
archives, and lessons learned. Explore the Recent Projects, Space Team Online, to join
the men and women who make the Shuttle fly and learn about their diverse and
exciting careers. Peek behind the scenes as these folks train the astronauts, prepare the
Shuttle between missions, launch the Shuttle, successfully execute the flight from
Mission Control, and safely land the Shuttle and return it to the Kennedy Space
Center. Or take a look at NeurOn, a project that focuses on the NeuroLab space
shuttle mission which will study the brain. NeurOn includes a television component
airing on PBS stations in 40 states.

Passport to Knowledge

http://passport.ivv.nasa.gov/

Passport to Knowledge (PTK) is an ongoing series of "electronic field trips to scientific
frontiers." Supported by the National Science Foundation, NASA, public television,
and other collaborators, it encourages and permits students to interact with real science, real scientists, real locations, and real time. Passport to Knowledge uses broadcast TV, videotape, e-mail, the World Wide Web, and hands-on discovery activities so
students can actively simulate the science seen on camera and online in their own
classrooms. It's flexible so that even teachers with limited time and technology can
participate. Targeted at middle school students, activities can be adapted up or down

in grade. They also provide connections to math, social studies, language arts, technology education, and other disciplines, while meeting the National Science Education standards. Online discussion groups provide teacher-to-teacher support, as well as interactive projects for student-with-student collaboration. Projects include Live From Antarctica and Live From Antarctica 2, Live from the Stratosphere, Live from the Hubble Space Telescope, and Live from Mars.

TIP

An easy way to keep abreast of the latest projects is to point your browser to the Information Searcher Online at http://www. infosearcher.com. Click on Pipeline, an online column highlighting the best telecollaborative projects for K–12.

OnlineClass

http://www.onlineclass.com

OnlineClass creates original K–12 programming for the Internet, delivering a planned, organized, and moderated e-mail/Web learning experience. Here you'll find live, original interactive programming materials—the "hook"—for the interdisciplinary teaching experience you want to have! Program selection includes the following:

> Mythos: Zeus Speaks!
>
> Blue Ice: Focus On Antarctica
>
> Rivers of Life: Mississippi Adventure
>
> The North American Quilt: A Living Geography Project
>
> Self* Expressing *Earth
>
> DoodleOpolis: Adventures in Urban Architecture

Each project includes a moderated e-mail discussion, access to online guests and/or special interactive features, a student showcase on the Web, guided Web research, a print teachers' resource guide, and related classroom activities.

Sites Alive

http://www.sitesalive.com

Sponsored by Ocean Challenge, students go on field trips exploring the world. They invite others, in schools and at home, to join them on their live, semester-long learning experience. You can read their journals, essays, question and answers, and hear their audio reports, see photos, and read their bios. Students in grades three through nine go on virtual field trips to the last remaining rainforest of Australia with Rainforest Live, or in the vibrant coral reefs of the Caribbean Sea with Ocean Live or on a voyage around the world onboard the tall ship *Concordia* with Class Afloat Live. Participating students experience and learn from the wonder and discovery shared by student researchers around the world through travel journals, photos, questions and answers, and audio. Information is sent via satellite and the Internet to Ocean Challenge headquarters in Boston, Massachusetts, and is available on this Web site and featured in newsletters published during the school year. (See Figure 5.7.)

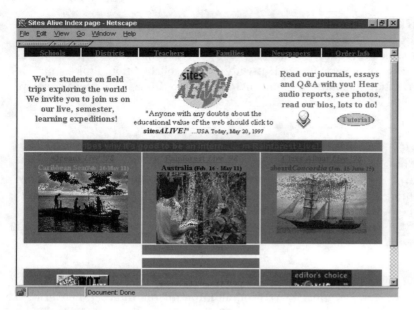

Figure 5.7
Web site for Sites Alive virtual field trips.

Turner Adventure Learning

http://www.turner.com/tesi

Sponsored by CNN and the Turner Education Series, Turner Adventure Learning brings students on diverse electronic field trip adventures that feature interdisciplinary activities. View past and present projects and adventures via the Electronic Field Trips link from the home page. For an interesting twist on learning, look at the Baseball Project where students can take a virtual trip to the Atlanta Braves Spring Training Camp in Palm Beach, Florida. They meet the players and coaches who use math and science to improve the game, see demonstrations of baseball maneuvers and how different sciences are applied, and apply a variety of disciplines to the game of baseball. Each adventure includes an overall project description, registration information, an explanation of the interactive component, and detailed curriculum and learning objectives for each phase of the learning adventure. A Learning Kit, which includes a preview program and a teacher's resource book, can be purchased for a fee.

ADVANCED STRATEGY
Develop your own project! Check out this site for help in designing a telecollaborative project at http://www.gsn.org/teach/articles/design. project.html. But first, join an already established project to get your feet wet. Keep a journal of what you like and don't like and suggestions on how to improve the project. Build on that experience to develop your project.

More Projects

To keep up-to-date on telecollaborative activities, logon on to these sites.

Hilites
http://www.gsn.org/teach/list/hilites.html

Information Searcher Online
http://www.infosearcher.com

NickNacks
http://www1.minn.net/~schubert/NickProjects.html

Pitsco's Launch to On-Line Collaborative Projects
http://askanexpert.com/p/collab.html

NickNacks offers an e-mail update service. Subscribe to NickNack's Update.

WEAVING A WEB-BASED CURRICULUM
How do you integrate the Internet into your curriculum? Take a CyberTour and learn some strategies that incorporate Internet resources and use the unique features of the Internet to motivate, involve, and challenge students to be active learners.

STRATEGY 5—LOOK AT WHAT OTHER EDUCATORS ARE DOING

It isn't always necessary to start from scratch when developing a new curriculum. Sometimes it's better to look at curriculum units and lesson plans that other educators have developed and adapt them for your use. When you are working collaboratively with teachers to develop new units incorporating information literacy skills and technology, it's helpful to have samples of successful units or projects to jumpstart the planning session.

ICONnect Prize for Collaboration Through Technology (ICPrize)
http://www.ala.org/ICONN/minigran.html

The American Association of School Librarians' technology initiative, ICONnect, has a web page highlighting the winners of the ICONnect ICPrize.

Collaborative teams of school library media specialists and classroom teachers can apply for ICONnect ICPrize of $1000 to be used toward the purchase of technology for use in the library media center or to support travel for the team to attend a state or national conference. The school library media specialist applying for the ICONnect ICPrize must be a member of ALA/AASL. Read over the description of the project and also the criteria. Both can act as a guide in curriculum development of new or adapted units.

Following is a list of recent ICONnect ICPrize winners and the projects they developed:

Jo Ann Wahrman, school library media specialist

Sharon Palmquist, participating teacher—Goodland High School, Goodland, Kansas.

Examining common characteristics of assassinations throughout history can be a bridge to understanding events in Shakespeare's *Julius Caesar*. By researching different victims of assassination, student groups learned the assassinated person's background, why he or she was targeted, how and by whom the assassination was carried out, and what impact the person's death had on history. Using journalism techniques, students shared their information. Through discussion afterward, students made generalizations about motives and results of assassinations as well as types of victims and the morally complex roles of assassins.

Constance Vidor, librarian

Ellen Baru, technology coordinator

John Lawes, social studies teacher—The Cathedral School, New York.

As a culmination of their study of the ancient Roman Empire, the sixth-grade students used books, CD-ROM, and a variety of preselected Web sites to research different types of ancient Roman people, including slaves, gladiators, bath attendants, cooks, senators, actors, architects, farmers, and aristocratic women. The final product was a Hyperstudio stack in which each student assumed a role and shared information about his or her life.

Nelda Brangwin, school library media specialist

Christine Hauser, first grade teacher—Cherry Valley Elementary School, Duvall, Washington.

As a part of the first grade social studies unit, students are introduced to different cultures. When studying Japan, students exchanged drawings of favorite foods, holidays, favorite toys, and families with students in Oanan Elementary School in Tsukuba City, Ibaraki Prefecture, Japan. A "big book" was written on Japan, and the unit culminated with a Web page housed on each school's Internet home page: "A Day in the Life of a First Grader in Washington State" and "A Day in the Life of a First Grader in Japan."

Shelby Bivens, library/media specialist

David Mittel, language arts teacher—Kyrene Middle School, Tempe, Arizona.

The unit was developed as a research and presentation project. Students researched favorite authors and read their books. Afterwards, students organized their information into a storyboard and used PowerPoint software to develop a presentation with text, downloaded Internet graphics, and special effects. Students shared their author studies with students from other language arts classes. This project increased students' understanding of various uses of technology which included Internet and CD-ROM searches. Students also improved skills in writing, research, public speaking, and using technology for presentations.

Carolyn Karis, school library media specialist

Elizabeth Wade, French class teacher—Urban School of San Francisco.

The Francophone African study unit culminated in oral French presentations that provided high school French students with context for reading francophone African literature. Students researched individual countries to gain background in the history and culture of former French colonies in Africa. The students used French and English Internet resources,

CD-ROM, books, and videos. This project increased students' cultural awareness and their comprehension of the richness of francophone literature, their communication skills, their critical use of information resources, and their French-speaking abilities.

Lesson Plans

Lesson plan collections are also a good resource. Listed as follows are the best ones on the Web. Many of these sites, such as AskERIC, list other lesson plan collections to explore. As you read over the lesson plans, identify those that use technology and have students actively using information skills.

AskERIC
http://ericir.syr.edu/Virtual/Lessons/

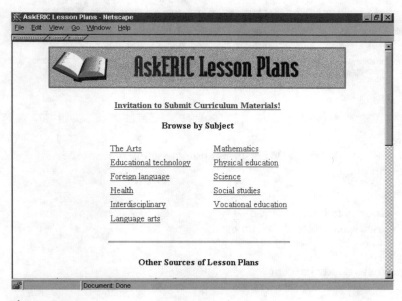

Figure 5.8
Visit AskERIC for sample lesson plans you can use with your students.

Encarta Lesson Plan Collection
http://encarta.msn.com/schoolhouse/lessons/default.asp

ILT Web: Live Text, Lesson Plans
http://www.ilt.columbia.edu/k12/livetext/curricula/general/index.html

GEM
http://geminfo.org/

MCREL
  http://www.mcrel.org/connect/plus/index.html

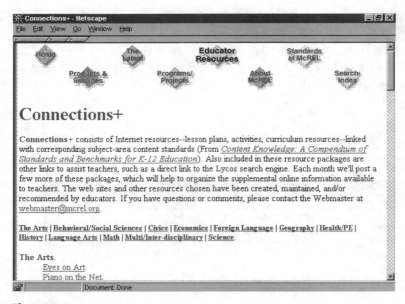

Figure 5.9
The MCREL Connections Web site is another excellent resource
for lesson plans.

Pitsco's Launch to Lesson Plans
  http://www.pitsco.com/p/lesson.html

Study Web
  http://www.studyweb.com

Chapter 6

Resources for Active Learning

The Internet can be used to change a passive learning environment into an active, constructivist one. Students are given the opportunity to make sense of information, construct their own meaning, and be involved in their own learning. The Web offers new kinds of resources that fit naturally with these instructional goals. This chapter focuses on using Internet resources to support student learning. Unlike the previous chapter where we used structured approaches (such as WebQuests and telecollaborative projects), this approach focuses on identifying the unique features of Internet resources and examining how they can have an impact on the teaching and learning process.

A few of the resources described take advantage of the immediacy of information found on the Web (such as full-text news databases). Another resource uses a high degree of interactivity to involve and motivate students (such as those listed as "Active Learning " sites and "Asking an Expert" sites). Still other resources utilize the technology to its fullest with live cameras. The Web resources collected in this chapter reflect both the traditional library program (locating answers to reference questions and using primary resources) and the innovative, customized news sources, like PointCast. These resources are offered as suggestions to help you effectively integrate the Web into your library and your school's curriculum and to view the Web with a fresh new approach to technology/curriculum integration.

As you become more familiar with the Web and explore its rich resources on your own, look at a Web page for its content relevance to the curriculum. Whenever I visit a new Web site I target specific curriculum content and concepts, comparing the content on the Web page to what is taught in the various curriculum areas. Next, I look for any unique features in the content, functions, and design. Finally, I consider its ability to create an active learning experience. How can kids use this page? How can they interact with its content and maybe even contribute to its content? How can I use this resource to enhance the curriculum and student learning?

Web resources are unique. Consider these points when using them.

URLs Change Daily. The Web is constantly changing and growing and, unfortunately, Web pages change their addresses or sometimes disappear all together. You may get the message "Unable to locate the server. Does not have DNS entry." To troubleshoot the URL, try deleting the subdirectories and logging on the main directory page. Perhaps the page you want has been moved to another directory and you can locate it from the main home page. Try logging on to the following Web site. Since there is nothing available at this address, first delete "articles.keys.html" to see if you get a listing of articles. Then delete "articles" and search on that page. Continue deleting sections of the URL until you are on the main home page of the organization.

> main directory/sub-directories
> http://www.gsn.org/teach/articles/index.html

Look for the address of the Webmaster on the main home page. E-mail the Webmaster and ask about the information you are seeking. Next, try going to Yahoo or AltaVista and search by keywords from the title of the Web page or content.

Systems Go Down.   Be prepared for your system to crash or go off line as the class is walking into the library. You might want to download a Web site ahead of time using an off-line browser (such as Web Wacker) that allows you to save Web pages (including text, graphics, and html links) directly to your hard drive. Download a demo of Web Wacker at http://207.245.226.222/text/itool.htm. If you decide to use Web Wacker, it's a good idea to e-mail the site you plan to capture and ask permission. State what you are going to use the site for and the time period you plan to use it.

Explore Good Sites.   As you search the Web for information on specific topics and you come across a Web site you particularly like, stay and look around. Most likely you will find other information, projects, or links that are helpful. Think curriculum and active learning and always be on the prowl for good sites.

Bookmark and Organize URLs.   It's very easy to forget where you found a particular Web site no matter how much you backtrack. Be sure to bookmark sites that look valuable; you can always delete the bookmark later when you are organizing them into folders. In Netscape Navigator, click on Add Bookmark, then Bookmark Properties to write a brief description of the site.

Entice Faculty to the Web.   Send URLs of good Web sites you have found to faculty members that you think might be interested. In Netscape Navigator use the Control key and M key to have an e-mail message window appear. Cut and paste the Web site URL into Message and include a few sentences describing the content or how it could be used with their curriculum.

WEB SITES FOR ACTIVE LEARNING

When kids talk about playing basketball, football, or soccer, they describe intricate plays at length, with enormous animation. They rarely give a play-by-play account of the coach's instructions. The fun and exhilaration comes with "doing" the sport, not listening to how to do it or how others have done it. Real learning takes place when one is actively involved—shooting from the sideline, missing by an inch, analyzing how to perfect the shot, shooting again, and making the basket!

Web sites that give students an opportunity to be personally included, to "do science" to "be a writer" or to "be an artist," automatically involve them intellectually. Such project-based learning gets their creative juices flowing, providing opportunities to apply and practice skills. This type of instruction addresses kids' proficiencies and stresses intrinsic motivation while it encourages them to determine what to work on. It accepts them as experts in reference to their needs. The following Web sites give kids a chance to do real-world things, have real-world experiences. They empower students to be social activists, zoo interns, mystery writers, investigators, dreamers, environmentalists, artists, poets, stock market investors, geographers, scientists, historians, and more. A few examples are listed here. A full list of "Active Learning" Web sites can be found in appendix A.

Nonprofit Prophets

http://www.kn.pacbell.com/wired/prophets/index.html

A telecommunications/community action project that challenges groups of students to investigate a problem that they see in the world and create a World Wide

Web Resource page that teaches the world about the problem. It challenges them to become prophets—people gifted with more than ordinary moral insight who stand out as effective leaders for a cause. Students in ninth and tenth grade English, social studies, science, health, and applied technology classes serve as core teams investigating a problem in local or global communities that they think needs fixing. Students in other grades can work as consultants, experts, researchers, data gatherers, technologists, or graphic artists to help the core team. Professionals from around the world contribute expertise, feedback, and support to the student teams as they create the projects. The Web site provides guidelines, templates, and samples to get started.

Arctica

http://www.gene.com/ae/arc/

Arctica, a mystery revealed in weekly episodes, invites students to read background, examine clues, and submit guessed solutions. It is one of Access Excellence Science Mysteries sponsored by Genentech. Its purpose is to inspire high school students and the world at large to develop skills needed to solve mysteries—not on paper, but in the infinite variety of real-life mysteries waiting just outside the classroom door. Students can compete to solve a portion of the Arctica mystery at the end of each episode. They electronically submit the answer to the question at the end of the episode, and an explanation of the solution. Prize winners are selected from all the correct entries. Usually the prizes are T-shirts, mouse pads, bookmarks, or posters. You can visit two other science mysteries, The Blackout Syndrome and River of Venom. (See Figure 6.1.)

Figure 6.1
Try to solve the mystery of Arctica! Episodes appear weekly and students can submit guessed solutions via e-mail.

Children's Express

http://www.ce.org/welcome.html

This Web site is designed for active participation by students so that the concerns and voices of children and teens are heard, respected, and acted upon. Students in grades 10 through 12 serve as news reporters, post messages, and participate in news pools and listservs in this 20-year-old news service produced by kids. Students can participate on their Web site in addition to submitting story ideas and becoming online reporters. Every month Children's Express posts articles written by one of the six News Bureaus and encourages students to respond. They regularly conduct polls about youth issues in the news and share results. This an excellent interdisciplinary opportunity.

The Case

http://www.thecase.com/thecase/

Create your own mystery, read a chilling story, amaze your friends with magic tricks—all on the Web. The Case, a premiere mystery site on the Web, offers free high quality weekly mysteries. A special section for kids features scary stories, magic tricks, and contests. Mini-mysteries every week encourage students to submit solutions and create and submit original stories. They are an entertaining way to help teach critical thinking and deductive reasoning. A special section, Learning with Mysteries, includes information and resources for educators. (See Figure 6.2.)

Figure 6.2
Another mystery Web site is The Case. Here students can solve mysteries or create and submit their own.

Kids As Global Scientists

http://onesky.engin.umich.edu/kgs98/index.980116.html

This Web site focuses on using the Internet in a middle school weather curriculum. Students collect their own weather data, correspond with peers and meteorologists worldwide and real-time, and view archival satellite weather imagery.

InvestSmart

http://library.advanced.org/10326/

In this interactive stock market simulation, each player is given $100,000 to invest in over 5,000 companies along with tips, portfolio set-ups, and research capability.

Energy Net Community Web

http://www.energynet.net/

Energy Net is an innovative network science project in which students evaluate their school's heating and lighting systems, and then share their data over the Internet. Students form scientific research communities in which they learn about the production, cost, and management of the energy upon which both their school and their society depend. EnergyNet students use technology, teamwork, and skills from a variety of disciplines to solve real-life energy problems, research solutions, and influence change. Students form teams to evaluate and influence the management of their school's energy use by conducting physical energy audits, collecting and analyzing data, researching possible solutions on the Internet, and presenting the most effective solutions to their School Board for action. A well-developed, authentic science class project!

DEVELOP YOUR OWN ACTIVE LEARNING SITE

Consider setting up a Web site that will offer your students an opportunity to do authentic tasks. Following are two good examples of school Web sites. They differ from the previous sites in that they have only their own students' work, which makes the site easier to manage. It will help give additional purpose to your Web site while using it as curriculum integration tool.

What did you do in the war, Grandma?

http://www.stg.brown.edu/projects/WWII_Women/tocCS.html

An excellent example of a Web-based oral history project, this Oral History of Rhode Island Women before and during the Second World War was written by students. It includes a World War II timeline, a "streaming audio" presentation of one of the original interviews, and links to oral history resources, articles, bibliography, and reference pages. (See Figure 6.3.)

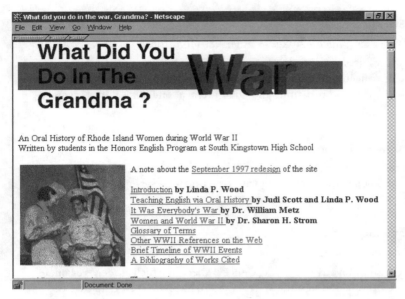

Figure 6.3
What Did You Do in the War, Grandma? is a World War II oral history project.

Princeton High School's Virtual Museum

http://www.prs.k12.nj.us/Schools/PHS/History/World_History/

Teach kids to be art critics. The Virtual Museum, originally written by teachers but now added on to by students, contains a collection of art appreciation/history lessons on representative works from European, African, American, Native American, Islamic, and Asian Art.

UNIQUE INTERNET RESOURCES

Introduce students to the unique resources the Internet has to offer, such as personalized news and information services, full-text databases, electronic text, and electronic journals. The following resources not only extend the school library's collection but also broaden students' understanding of the Web as a new information resource. Often these resources can be woven into the curriculum to locate specific information or as a strategy to keep current on specific topics. The faculty will also find these resources very helpful to access professional and personal topics.

Customized News and Information Services

PointCast

http://www.pointcast.com

The PointCast Network delivers news and information, personalized to your specifications, directly to your desktop. Using their software, which can be downloaded free from http://www.pointcast.com, PointCast automatically updates your news on a regular basis. Get local, national, and international news; stock information; industry updates; weather updates; sports scores; and more from leading sources like CNN, *The Wall Street Journal* and *The New York Times.* To receive your updates the Pointcast Network allows you to set up an automatic update schedule. Or, you can manually click on the Update button.

PointCast College, a special edition designed for students, includes U-Wire. This contains daily news written by student reporters and selected from over 120 campus newspapers with a focus on college news, campus life, careers, and opinions. In addition to news from popular sources like CNN, *The New York Times, Time* and *People* magazines, ZDNet, and hundreds more, the PointCast College Network features five news and information channels with special campus appeal.

CRAYON

http://crayon.net

CRAYON, which stands for *CReAte Your Own Newspaper,* is a tool for managing news sources on the Internet and the Web. It uses a newspaper analogy to organize the periodical information you are most interested in. It easy to set up: connect to http://crayon.net. Then click on CReAte Your Own Newspaper, enter your e-mail address as your login ID, name your newspaper, and give it a motto. You are now ready to choose your news categories. Within each section you choose the resource you want included in that section. The number of resources varies—the U.S. News section has 20 newspapers to choose from; Science has 13 choices, Politics has 9, and Sports has over 30. As you finish a section, click on the Next button to continue. Or stop by clicking on the Create this newspaper now button. The sections include: U.S. News, Regional and Local News, World News, Politics as Usual, Editorial and Opinions, Weather Conditions and Forecasts, Business Report, Information and Technology Report, Health and Fitness Roundup, Arts and Entertainment, Sports Day, Snippets Corner, Funny Page, Tabloid Page, and New and Cool Web Sites. You can modify or change your choices at any time by clicking on the Modify button. You can access your page by bookmarking your newspaper address or by connecting to the CRAYON site and entering your e-mail address. (See Figure 6.4.)

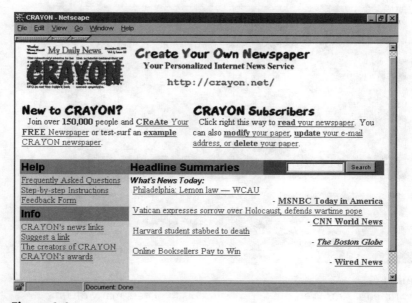

Figure 6.4
CRAYON allows students to create their own newspapers, learning about news events as they go.

ICONnect
Learn how to effectively integrate the Internet into the curriculum. Sign up for two free online courses on the ICONnect Web site, Curriculum Integration Using the Web and Integrating the Internet into the Elementary Curriculum. Learn the whys and hows of using Internet and Web-related material in the curriculum and how to make the integration successful.

Free Full-Text Databases

Pathfinder

http://www.pathfinder.com/welcome/

Time Warner's Pathfinder provides access to more than 150,000 pages for over 90 of the largest news, information and entertainment magazines including *Time, Money, Sports Illustrated, Entertainment Weekly, People,* and *Fortune.* Its opening page resembles one of the large Internet online services, offering links to a wealth of Internet resources. Students can search for information either through the main search utility or go directly to specific magazines, such as *Time* or *Fortune,* and search. The Help section explains how to use Boolean operators. To search for articles on sports and steroids, use the & character, as in sports & anabolic steroids. To exclude a term, use an explanation point, as in burgundy! wine. This will allow you to find information on the Burgundy region of France and exclude any information on wine. There is also a great site, *Time for Kids,* at http://www.pathfinder.com/@ @pD03XUAVR*21azq/TFK/. (See Figure 6.5.)

Figure 6.5
The *Time for Kids* Web site allows students to access many of *Time* magazine's news stories.

ZD Net

http://www3.zdnet.com/zdnn/

ZD Net, from Ziff Davis Publishing Company, offers Page One, the ZDNet News Channel. Similar to Pathfinder, it offers current news, world headlines, market views, sports, and more. This site is particularly useful for searching computer and Internet-related magazines such as *Computer Life, Computer Shopper, PC Computing, PC Magazine, PC Week, Mac User, Mac WEEK, Yahoo Internet Life, Family PC, Electronic Gaming Monthly,* and more.

Digital Libraries and E-Zines

Project Gutenberg

http://www.promo.net/pg/

Project Gutenberg, established in 1971 at the University of Illinois by Michael Hart, is an online database of electronic texts. Beginning with The Declaration of Independence as the first e-text, Project Gutenberg's goal was to make information, books, and other material available to the general public in forms that the vast majority of the computers, programs, and people can easily read, use, quote, and search. From the home page you can search by title and author for almost 300 printed works. The home page also contains information on how to sign up for their newsletter, how to stay informed on their progress, the copyright, the history of the project, and ways in which the public can support the project.

Alex: a Catalog of Electronic Texts on the Internet

http://www.lib.ncsu.edu/staff/morgan/alex/alex-index.html

Alex was an informal research project. Its purpose was to explore the possibilities of creating catalogs of Internet-based electronic texts. Originally conceived by Hunter Monroe in 1993–94, the catalog contains roughly 2,000 entries. Maintenance and continued development of the Alex catalog has been suspended due to lack of funds, but access is still available.

Wiretap

http://wiretap.spies.com

Wiretap is run as a free public service to provide electronic text to citizens of the Internet, sort of a warehouse of e-texts. As one of the earliest e-text repositories, there are thousands of links to this site. Choose Electronic Books to view ten pages of single spaced titles of books. This site includes White House press releases, historical documents, and Usenet e-text archives.

The On-line Books Page

http://www.cs.cmu.edu/books.html

The On-line Books Page is a directory of books that can be freely read on the Internet. It has an index of thousands of online books, listing of significant directories, and archives divided into General, Foreign Language, Specialty (i.e., Religion, Poetry, Children, Computers, Women, etc.), and special exhibits. You

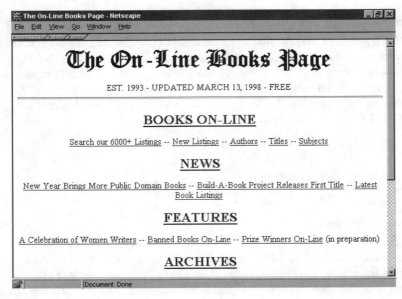

Figure 6.6
The On-Line Books Page is an index of thousands of books that can be read on the Internet.

can search the collection by title or author and also look at the New Listing for current acquisitions. (See Figure 6.6.)

The World Wide Web Virtual Library: Electronic Journals

http://www.edoc.com/ejournal/

The Virtual Journal maintained by WILMA, Web Information List Management Agency, includes nine categories: Academic and Reviewed Journals, College or University, E-mail, Magazines or Newspapers, Politics, Print, Publishing Topics, Business/Finance, and Other Resources. You can access entries in the catalog either by searching the full-text of long descriptions, short descriptions, and titles or by browsing through any one of the nine categories.

Internet WebZines

http://wwwscout.cs.wisc.edu/scout/toolkit/publications/internetweb.html

Eight Internet Webzines (publications that appear only on the Internet) and five Internet magazines (print magazines that also have Web sites) are listed on this site. They can also be accessed from this site—the place to find the latest information about the Internet and the Web. Brief annotations describing the content and searching capability are given.

E-zine List

http://www.meer.net/~johnl/e-zine-list/

John Labovitz maintains this definitive list of e-zines. It contains information on over 1,300 e-zines.

ICONnect

Need a list of good Web sites for K–12? Logon to ICONnect's Curriculum Connections section. Divided by curriculum, these Web sites have been identified for use in K–12 curriculum and have been evaluated and annotated by school librarians. Print them out and share them with your faculty.

REFERENCE ON THE WEB

Take a tour through the Web to view unique Web resources that support and enhance curriculum. Look at the valuable primary resources, curriculum collections with a twist, in-depth reference sites, and more

USE PRIMARY SOURCES

Using primary source material in the curriculum is an excellent way to engage students with the real issues of history and to offer them different perspectives to analyze, compare, and argue. The process of using primary sources helps students develop the knowledge, skills, and analytical abilities they will need to be information literate in the twenty-first century. With the advent of the Internet, and especially the Web, locating and accessing primary source documents has become easier.

The Library of Congress' American Memory Page includes a Learning Page devoted to helping educators use primary sources. It provides a framework to assist educators in using primary source materials in the curriculum and includes four sections: Rationale for Using Primary Sources, Selecting Sources, Organizing Instruction, and Activities for the Instructional Cycle. Following is a listing of primary sources found on the Web. After reading the suggestions on the Learning Page, look at History in the Raw on the National Archives and Records Administration Web site which provides a rationale for using primary sources in the curriculum.

Primary Source Web Sites

American Memory Site

http://rs6.loc.gov/amhome.html

The American Memory Project is an on-line resource compiled by the Library of Congress National Digital Library Program. Millions of the Library's unique American history collections are being digitized and make freely available to teachers, students, and the general public over the Internet.

Emory Law Library: Electronic Reference Desk

http://www.law.emory.edu/LAW/refdesk/country/us/docs.html

This Web site contains a collection of links to historical documents such as the Federalist Papers, Declaration of Independence, Magna Carta, Martin Luther King, Jr. Papers Project, White House Press Releases, and much more. (See Figure 6.7.)

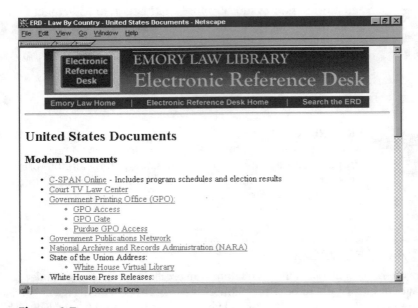

Figure 6.7
The Emory Law Library Electronic Reference Desk provides easy access to links with many important historical documents.

Eurodocs: Western European Primary Historical Documents

http://library.byu.edu/~rdh/eurodocs/

This site contains links to Western European primary historical documents that shed light on key historical happenings within their respective countries and within the broadest sense of political, economic, social, and cultural history.

Historical Text Archive

http://www.msstate.edu/Archives/History

The Historical Text Archive (HTA) originated in 1990 in response to historians' need to have an electronic storage and retrieval site and to demonstrate the advantages of such sites for the study and teaching of history. It provides original material, links to other sites (such as Oklahoma's historical document collection), and electronic reprints of books. It's organized by geography/nations and topics.

National Archives and Records Administration

http://www.nara.gov/exhall/

This site is an excellent resource for unique primary source material, including posters from World War II, a behind-the-scenes story of the meeting between Richard Nixon and Elvis Presley, and a police report on the assassination of Abraham Lincoln. Featured documents include a Japanese Surrender document, a letter for Jackie Robinson, and the Marshall Plan. (See Figure 6.8.)

Figure 6.8
To go right to the source (that is, the primary source), check out the National Archives and Records Administration Web site.

U.S. Historical Documents

http://www.law.uoknor.edu/ushist.html

This site contains an excellent chronology of U.S. historical documents, ranging from the pre-Colonial era to the present.

ELECTRONIC REFERENCE SOURCES

Introduce students to the online reference world. Whether they are searching for ready answers to reference questions, more in-depth knowledge on topics to research, basic background data, or keywords for a full-text database search, Internet reference sources can provide the needed information. Following are a few examples of good Web reference sites. A full listing can be found in appendix B. Use these sites to develop your library home page. Encourage students to become proficient in accessing and searching these electronic resources.

There is a wealth of reference material on the Internet. If you are looking for biographical information, the first place to stop is Biography at http://www.biography.com/ which includes a searchable text of 15,000 entries from *The Cambridge Biographical Encyclopedia* along with video and audio clips. Or perhaps the Notable Citizens of the *Planet Earth Biographical Dictionary* at http://www.tiac.net/users/parallax/ might help. It contains brief biographical statements on over 18,000 people from ancient times to the present day. If the individual is a poet, try the Academy of American Poets at http://www.poets.org/. If the person is a Nobel Prize winner, then it's easy. The Nobel Prize Internet Archive at http://www.almaz.com/ will be right on target with its searchable database of past Nobel Laureates, organized by prize and year. Entries include brief biographical information and varied links to related WWW sites. An entertaining, current information source about celebrities can be found at CelebSite http://www.celebsite.com/.

For students researching companies, try the Dow Jones Industrial Average Database at http://ipl.org/ref/stocks/. This site is maintained by the Internet Public Library, which provides quick and easy access to corporate and stock information for the companies in the DJIA. The 1998 Fortune 500 Web site at http://pathfinder.com/fortune/1997/specials, courtesy of *Fortune* magazine, offers detailed information, including rankings, on the Fortune 500 and the Global 500 companies. Business and stock market news is also available.

For the latest information on educational standards, logon to the Putnam Valley School District's Educational Standards Web site at http://putwest.boces.org/standards.html. It's the best place to go when you need information about national or state standards, documents, or curriculum frameworks in any subject area. And, of course, there is the ERIC Clearinghouse at http://ericir.syr.edu. To search for educational resources by keyword, follow the link to "search Eric database." It includes citations and abstracts for documents and journal articles published since 1989. (See Figure 6.9.)

TheWebcontainseverythingfromRhymingDictionariesathttp://www.link.cs.cmu.edu/dougb/rhyme-doc.html to Foreign Language Dictionaries at http://www.june29.com//HLP/. Census data can be found at http://icg.fas.harvard.edu/~hist1651/census/.

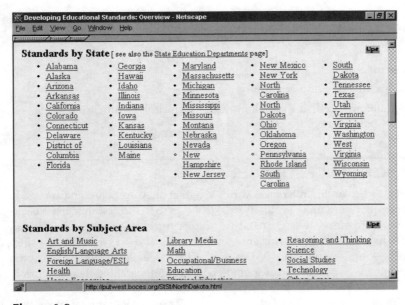

Figure 6.9
If you are looking for information about national or state education standards, try the Putnam Valley School District's Educational Standards Web site.

There is also an interactive atlas like MapQuest at http://www.mapquest.com which provides city-to-city driving directions for the U.S., and parts of Canada, information on Associations on the Net can be found at http://ipl.org/ref/AON/ and Geographic Names at http://www-nmd.usgs.gov/www/gnis/gnisform.html. Teach your students to search efficiently using these sites along with the other reference sources in appendix B. Most importantly, though, teach them how to evaluate the reference sources. They need to know when to use an electronic source and when it is best to use a print or CD-ROM source. Have students compare the Web version of Quotations (1904) and the print version (1997). They will quickly realize that famous quotes by Martin Luther King, Jr., and John F. Kennedy are not online. (See Figure 6.10.)

Figure 6.10
Instead of asking for directions, next time plan your trip across town or across the country with the help of MapQuest, an interactive atlas.

ONLINE EXPERTS

One of the unique capabilities of the Internet is its ability to put kids in touch with experts. Students can send an e-mail message to a scientist, a stock market trader, an artist, a zoologist, a fitness trainer, a fly fishing expert, a lawyer, or even a bubble expert. A comprehensive site with links to hundreds of experts is Pitsco's Ask an Expert page. AskERIC, funded by the U.S. Department of Education, answers questions on the theory or practice of education. KidsConnect Question and Answer Service helps kids learn how to locate information on the Internet.

Pitsco's Ask an Expert

http://www.askanexpert.com/askanexpert/index.html

Select from 12 categories with over 300 Web sites and e-mail addresses where you can find experts to answer your questions from the Amish lifestyles to facts about zoo keeping. Ask an Expert is a directory of links to people who have volunteered their time to answer questions and Web pages that provide information. Categories include Science/Technology, Health, Recreation/Entertainment, International/Cultural, Money/Business, Law, Career/Industry, Internet/Computer, Education/Personal Development, Resources, Arts, and Religion.

AskERIC

http://ericir.syr.edu/Qa

Teachers, library media specialists, administrators, and others involved in education can send a message requesting information on the theory and practice. Within 48 hours a specialist will answer your e-mail with ERIC database searches, ERIC Digest, and Internet resources.

KidsConnect

http://www.ala.org/ICONN/AskKC.html

KidsConnect, a component of AASL's technology initiative, ICONnect, is a question and answer service to K–12 students on the Internet. KidsConnect helps students access and use the information on the Internet effectively and efficiently. Students send questions via e-mail or fill out a form on the KC Web page and receive help within two school days from specially trained school library media specialists. The focus is on helping kids learn how to use the Internet, so the answer will include strategies to allow students to find the information themselves. It's operated in partnership with the Information Institute of Syracuse, Syracuse University, and is underwritten by Microsoft Corporation. (See Figure 6.11.)

Encourage your students to logon on to the KC Web page at http://www.ala.org/ICONN/AskKC.html and fill out the form. (See Figure 6.12).

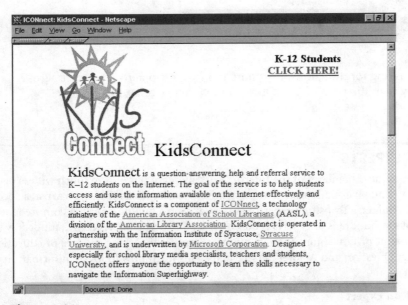

Figure 6.11
When students are stumped for an answer, have them look for help at KidsConnect, a question-answering help and referral service.

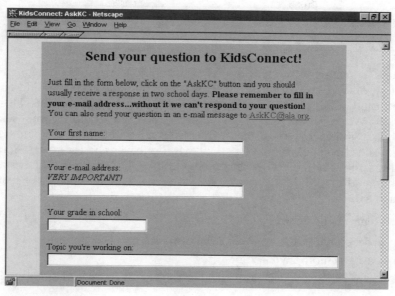

Figure 6.12
This site shows students how to submit a question to KidsConnect. The tips for finding the answer on the Internet (not the answer itself) will be received within two school days.

ICONnect
Become a KidsConnect volunteer. Get trained online via the Internet—be a member of a professional, innovative national project! The ICONnect Task Force is looking for school library media specialists interested in being trained as KidsConnect Volunteers. Go to http://www.ala.org/ICONN/kcvolunteer.html for more information.

KidsConnect Frequently Asked Questions

Point and click your way through the questions most often received at KidsConnect. They are grouped by subject headings, such as Astronomy, Biographies, Science, and News and also by the most popular Topics, such as Animal Rights, Presidents, Space Shuttle, Volcanoes, or Endangered Species. A few of the frequently asked questions are:

Where can I find biographies on the Internet and in books?

Where can I find current events on the Internet?

Why do leaves change color in the fall?

How do I find out about the space shuttle?

I'd like to know about different volcanoes in the world.

Where can I find information about different cultures?

How do I make a bridge out of toothpicks?

KIDSCONNECT Q & A

Q: Why do leaves change color in the fall?

A: Hi, that's a great question! I always enjoy watching leaves turn from green to red, yellow, orange, and brown. How does it all work? The Web sites and other resources listed in this message have some very interesting explanations. I first searched the World Wide Web using HotBot at: http://www.hotbot.com. I selected the choice "the exact words" to narrow my search and to limit the number of accurate results I will get. Then, I typed in "why do leaves change color?" You can try this same search on other search engines like AltaVista (http://altavista. digital.com) and Yahoo! (http://www.yahoo.com). You can also use other search terms, such as:

> "leaves change color"
>
> +leaves +autumn
>
> +leaves +chlorophyll +color

Here are some sites that can help you learn about leaves, chlorophyll (the substance that makes leaves green), and colors:

Elementary Level

1. Simply Science—Why do leaves change color in the fall?
   http://www.waterw.com/~science/october.html
   Read this page for an explanation of leaves changing color and for activities to help you learn about leaves.
2. Why Leaves Change Colors
   http://hillside.sowashco.k12.mn.us/95-96/Hammer/autumn/leaves/justinleaves/leavesj.html
   This Web page has great pictures of fall leaves and trees.
3. Why Leaves Change Color from Rosa Stewart Elementary
   http://www.tilc.com/academy/fall96/fall1/prac1.htm
   This page has a list of questions about leaves for students to answer by looking at different Web sites. Once you've done some reading about the topic, try to answer the questions on this page. You can share the questions and your answers with your friends, teachers, and parents.

Secondary Level

4. Why Leaves Change Color—The Physiological Basis
   http://hermes.ecn.purdue.edu:8001/http_dir/acad/agr/extn/agr/acspub/html/FNR/FNR-FAQ.html
   A professor from Purdue University answers the question in detail. If you have trouble understanding any of the words, ask an adult to help you.
5. Autumn Chemistry: Sunny Days, Cool Nights Trigger Fall Hues
   http://www.gateway-va.com/pages/science/backstry/1003main.htm
   This page is from an article in a newspaper (*Richmond Times-Dispatch*).

6. Why Leaves Change Color from SUNY College of Environmental Science and Forestry

   http://www.esf.edu/pubprog/brochure/leaves/leaves.htm

   This page has nice sketches of fall leaves and a good explanation of why leaves change color.

In order to find books to answer your question, I used the library catalog and the search term "leaves" and "seasons." The books I chose all have a table of contents and index to help me find what I want quickly. Ask your library media specialist to help you find the following books in your library or through interlibrary loan.

How Leaves Change by Sylvia A. Johnson (Lerner Natural Science Book)
How Trees Help Me by Bobbie Kalman and Janine Schaub (Primary Ecology Series)
Leaves: Their Amazing Lives and Strange Behavior by James Poling
Seasons by Illa Podendorf (A new true book)
Sunshine Makes the Seasons by Franklyn M. Branley (Let's read and find out science book)

If your library has a CD-ROM called "Information Finder," try a search using the word "leaves." You will find all kinds of topics and information related to leaves, color, seasons, and nature. Information from this CD can then be read and parts of it can be copied and pasted into a word processor to use in a report later on. If you're writing a report, make sure you cite all of your sources (including books, Web sites, CD-ROM sources, etc.). Your library media specialist and teacher can help you.

J.G.
KidsConnect Volunteer

KidsConnect also has a listing of favorite Web sites at http://www.ala.org/ICONN/kcfavorites.html.

GO LIVE WITH VIDEO INTERACTION: CU-SEEME AND LIVE CAMS

CU-SeeMe

CU-SeeMe is a free videoconferencing program available to anyone with a Windows or Macintosh computer and a connection to the Internet. It allows geographically separate students and educators to see and hear each other, across the world or across the classroom, with only a small, relatively inexpensive camera plugged into a personal computer. Students can participate in CU-SeeMe special events and projects sponsored by the Global Schoolhouse, Cornell University, and others on the Internet. Logon to Cornell University's CU-SeeMe Page at http://cu-seeme.cornell.edu/ to find out how to get connected, receive technical support and receive information on the latest session of "Ask the Scientist." Global School Net has a section devoted to CU-SeeMe at http://www.gsn.org/cu/index.html containing a directory of schools participating worldwide, the CU-SeeMe Educational Calendar, Spotlight Events, and links to more resources. (See Figures 6.13 and 6.14.)

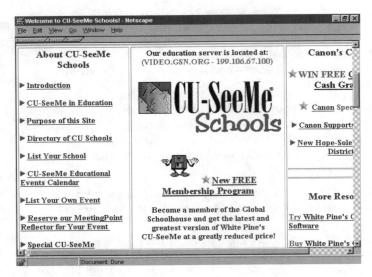

Figure 6.13
With a computer, an Internet connection, and an inexpensive camera, you and your
students can take part in video conferences through CU-SeeMe Schools.

Figure 6.14
Cornell University's CU-SeeMe page can help you get started on how to use
CU-SeeMe technology.

TIP
Point your browser to Cornell University's CU-SeeMe page to learn
how you can participate in a CU-SeeMe session. Information
includes hardware and software requirements, where you can go to
try it, and a discussion list to join.

Live Cams

Internet folklore weaves the story of computer programmers in Cambridge, England, setting up a live cam to see if the coffeepot was full before walking down the hall to get a refill. We have come a long way since then, but our fascination with viewing remote scenes is still strong. Live cams can help bring the curriculum alive in many ways. From social studies students observing different cultures in daily routines to language arts students writing essays on their observations, these experiences develop visual literacy and verbal articulation. Following is a list of live cam sites for you to explore.

Live Cam Web Sites

Tommy's List of Live Cam Worldwide

http://chili.rt66.com/ozone/cam.htm

This site contains an extensive listing of cam sites by state or countries. Includes special weather links for each location, and real audio sound clips for international sites.

World Map of Live WWW Cameras

http://dove.mtx.net.au/~punky/World.html

This unique site featuring a world map with hot links to live cameras around the world has a Quality Cam Award Page highlighting the best Cams. Most sites concentrate on "outside" cameras but if an "inside" site has a view that is characteristic of the country it will be included. (See Figure 6.15.)

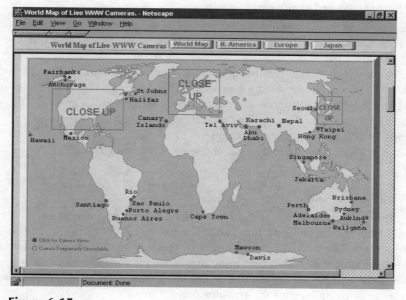

Figure 6.15
The World Map of Live WWW Cameras provides links with live cameras around the world.

Moscow Online

http://www.paratype.com/camera/camera.htm

Contains links to 27 world capitals and 17 lists of Web cams.

Earth Cam

http://earthcam.com

Links to Live Cam sites are divided into categories such as Business, Education, Scenic, Entertainment, Weird, and New sites. Extensive sites for a few major U.S. cities such as San Francisco, New York, and Philadelphia, are listed as well as traffic and weather Cams.

HOW TO FIND MORE SITES

The Web offers endless opportunities for incorporating resources into the curriculum; at times it can be overwhelming. Every time you research one site you find five more, then seven more, and the cycle goes on. After a while you will be able to discern quality and classify sites into meaningful categories for yourself. Following are a few sites that I think you will find very helpful. In addition to containing curriculum links (which most education sites do), these sites add a twist. They offer unique content or experiences such as a monthly update to help you learn about quality new sites, a listing of sites chosen by Q&A volunteers, Web sites developed by students to encourage new types of teaching and learning in the twenty-first century, and more. As you explore the sites, consider the unique resources that were presented in this chapter and continue to be on the lookout for more. As you visit them, be sure to bookmark. You'll want to go back to visit.

Blue Web'n Applications Library

http://www.kn.pacbell.com/wired/bluewebn/

This is a searchable database of outstanding Internet sites categorized by subject area, audience, and type (lessons, activities, projects, resources, references, and tools). Subscribe to the weekly e-mail updates to learn about the Hot Site of the Week and new Blue Web'n sites. Be sure to check out Fillamentality, a fill-in-the-blanks interactive Web site that guides you thorough picking a topic, searching the Web, gathering good Internet sites, and turning Web resources into activities appropriate for learners. Descriptions and sample of five activity structures designed for incorporating Internet resources in the curriculum are given: WebQuests, Treasure Hunt, Hot Lists, Scrapbook, and Sampler.

Ed's Oasis

http://www.edsoasis.org

The purpose of the Ed's Oasis site is to make the Internet easier and more rewarding to use with students. It includes The Treasure Zone, links to a collection of top-rated instructional sites which are organized by subject. Spotlight on Success highlights teachers who are using the Internet in their classroom activities. Evaluation Center allows you to examine the evaluation criteria and nominate sites to be considered for the Treasure Zone.

KidsConnect Favorites

http://www.ala.org/ICONN/kcfavorites.html

The KidsConnect volunteers have found these Web sites helpful in locating information to answer the hundreds of questions they receive each month. The KidsConnect Q&A Coordinator maintains and updates the list with help from the KC volunteers. It is divided into 27 categories for easy access.

ThinkQuest

http://io.advanced.org/ThinkQuest/quest.html

ThinkQuest, started in 1996, is a contest that challenges students from ages 12 to 19 to develop Web pages that help them, and other students, prepare for the twenty-first century. The winning teams' Web pages are arranged by category: Arts and Literature, Interdisciplinary, Science and Math, Social Sciences, and Sports and Health. Student competitors are challenged to harness the power of the Internet by developing Web sites that create new environments for teaching and learning. (See Figure 6.16.)

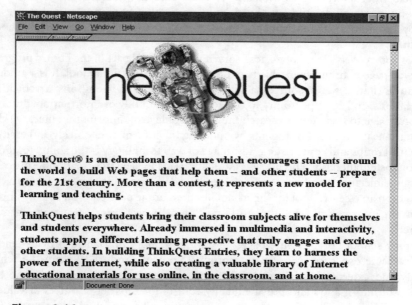

Figure 6.16
The Quest by ThinkQuest helps students develop their own Web pages.

Chapter 7

Developing a Library Home Page

The World Wide Web is changing the manner in which libraries provide services. As an integral part of the learning community, school libraries are developing Web sites to offer guidance in using Web resources and promote communications and research. The Web sites also offer continuing education and can be used as an instructional strategy.

For years school librarians have been information producers and creators of bibliographies, pathfinders, student handouts, and library displays. These guides, along with instruction, have helped students learn how to locate the best resource to meet their information needs. Creating library web pages is a new, dynamic way for school librarians to make Internet resources available to their students, faculty, and community. Library home pages guide students through the maze of information resources on the Internet by providing lists of evaluated, annotated Web sites that support the school's curriculum.

A school library Web site is not an accessory, but an essential part of the library program. A library web page is an indispensable twentieth century instructional tool. It is a guide to relevant, authoritative web resources, a space to share ideas and solutions, a vehicle for communications, and an opportunity to add to the current body of information. Students use the home page to learn how to search the Web and develop information literacy skills. School librarians use it to teach students by updating the information quickly and easily to target specific groups and content. One advantage of web technology is the ability to update information instantaneously. This allows school librarians to keep information resources as current as possible, updating library home pages on a daily basis, if necessary. Just as a card catalog has been an essential tool for the school library, a home page plays an equally important role in the information age library. A library home page supports teaching, learning, and research.

Developing school library home pages allows the school librarian to provide leadership and valuable expertise in organizing original content produced within the school community and external links to other sites on the Internet. Librarians have the best organization of information and provide quality control for Internet resources of value to the school community. The school librarian works with all curriculum areas, and teachers, administrators, and parents and can aid in the interaction and communication among groups.

Before you begin planning your own library home page, take some time to explore some pages that are already on the Internet. Look first at the organization; then review the most important sections, the graphics, the links, and the overall feel of the page. Bookmark the home pages so you can refer back to them.

WEB SITES LISTING SCHOOL LIBRARY HOME PAGES

School Libraries on the Web

>   http://www.voicenet.com/~bertland/libs.html

Peter Milbury's School Library and School Librarian Web Pages

>   http://www.cusd.chico.k12.ca.us/~pmilbury/lib.html

SCHOOL HOME PAGES

Web66 International WWW School Registry

>   http://web66.coled.umn.edu/schools.html

HotList of K–12 Internet School Site

>   http://rrnet.com/~gleason/k12.html

PLAN AHEAD

Take time to plan out the process of creating a home page. With each step you will need to make decisions starting from who is going to be involved and working through technical and design issues and maintenance considerations. A good place to start is with a brainstorming session with staff, teachers, an administrator, a parent, and a few students. The web page will be an important part of the library program and the planning and design of it should involve key players in the school community. Understanding each person's perspective will help you plan a more effective home page. Being involved in the development of the library home page will empower students, faculty, and parents to be more involved in and supportive of the library program.

   The Web is different from other information tools and needs careful consideration. It will have an impact on the library program, the staff, and the school community. The library staff must become familiar with electronic reference skills, learn new information search skills, and gain rudimentary knowledge of maintaining a web page. Students and teachers will need some instruction to become familiar with the Web and with home page navigation. Collection development will take place on the Web, identifying, evaluating, and making accessible Web sites on the virtual library page. Procedures will need to be developed for teachers and students to actively contribute to the development of external and internal Web links. Think about how the library home page can support your current library program. Don't think of it as "another thing to do," but rather as something that can help you get kids actively involved in learning search skills, provide ways to reach out to teachers and parents, and make the school library an integral part of the school's teaching and learning process. Use the library home page to encourage new collaborations and facilitate new communications in and out of the school community.

BUILDING YOUR LIBRARY WEB SITE
Why does every school library need a home page? Join a CyberTour and learn how school librarians are using home pages as instructional, communication, and public relations tools. Visit some of the best school library sites and learn how to develop a home page for your library.

DETERMINE THE PURPOSE AND GOALS

Once you have your planning group formed, start with writing a vision statement and decide on the purpose and goals of the library home page. Be clear about the relationship between the library home page and the school and district pages. The vision statement will help you focus on how you plan to use the library page to meet the library's information and instruction goals. As you articulate your vision, you need to simultaneously be thinking about how you will use the components of the home page to implement the vision. The purpose will be the same for most school libraries, but the primary focus and how the goals are achieved might be different. Identify user needs and decide what is most effective for your school library. The goals of a library home page might include guidance in the selection of Web sites and Web navigation, collection development, instruction, information, and public relations and communications.

Most school library home pages offer guidance to students and faculty in choosing the Web sites most relevant and appropriate to their curriculum and information needs. An essential part of the library home page is a section containing external links to evaluated, annotated Web sites. These sites are chosen because of their content relevance to the school curriculum. This will save students and faculty from needlessly wasting hours of searching on the Internet. Curriculum areas or meaningful topics can divide the external Web links, providing easy and quick access to relevant information. Faculty and students can take an active role in locating, evaluating, and briefly annotating new Web sites that they feel support the curriculum. This is a good opportunity to reach out to the faculty to set up a system for collaboratively maintaining the external Web links. Give a presentation at a faculty meeting explaining the key points of the evaluation form and invite the faculty members to join you in developing the library home page. Design a one-page form for them to submit suggested Web sites or ask them to submit their suggestions via e-mail.

You will need to look at your collection development policy and update it to include electronic resources and the use of a library home page. The World Wide Web is another resource in the school library, a unique information format to locate, organize, and make available to students and faculty. Use the library home page as an interactive, flexible collection development tool.

The library home page is an invaluable instructional resource to teach about the World Wide Web and its resources. When working with classes, small groups, or individuals, you can use the library home page to teach, pointing out specific sites and explaining strategies using examples from the home page. Specialized pages can be developed for a specific unit or project, listing recommended Web sites and documenting suggested search strategies and tips. Incorporate print handouts on the home page utilizing the hypertext power of the Web. Students can then access this page at a later time while working on the project.

Important polices and guidelines such as the Acceptable Use Policy (AUP), bibliographic style sheet, and a Web evaluation form should be easily accessible to students, faculty and parents whether they are in the school library, the classroom or at home. Information about the library program, staff, and services can also be included on the library page. Use it to help promote the school library, its philosophy, and its purpose. Show how it supports the teaching and learning process in the school.

A library home page can and should be interactive. Use it to communicate with students and faculty. Include your e-mail address and ask for suggestions to improve the page. Include a fill-in-the-blank form or a pop-up e-mail form for users to contribute suggestions to the external or internal curriculum links on the Web site. Think about how the library home page can be used to develop new collaborations that would be meaningful for students, faculty, or parents.

ADVANCED STRATEGY
For information on copyright, look at the Copyright Web site at http://www.benedict.com. "This site endeavors to provide real world, practical and relevant copyright information of interest to infonauts, netsurfers, webspinners, content providers, musicians, appropriation-ists, activists, infringers, outlaws, and law abiding citizens." Sections include Famous Copyright Infringements, Copyright Fundamentals, Fair Use, Public Domain, and more.

DECIDE ON THE CONTENT

When you create a virtual home page, you are creating a hypertext environment composed of both locally created documents and links to the files available on millions of host computers around the world. As you consider what information to include on your home page, be clear on whom the users will be and stay focused on what their information needs are. Most likely students and faculty will be the primary users, followed by administrators, parents, and community members. If the rest of the online world finds your Web site helpful, that's an added benefit, but not a primary concern when it comes to content considerations. Following is a listing of the different types of information you might want to include.

SUGGESTED CONTENT FOR LIBRARY HOME PAGE

1. Goals and Purpose of the virtual library page.
2. WebMaster's e-mail (hyperlinked to e-mail form).
3. Information about the school library: name of the library, address, phone, fax, staff, library philosophy, mission, hours, map, facility, special collections, services, library newsletter.
4. Current Information: New library materials, upcoming programs, additions and changes on the home page.
5. Curriculum Resource Guide: Listing of Web sites, evaluated, annotated (Curriculum areas and Reference).
6. Internal links to Student Produced Materials, student publications, book reviews, and subject reports or projects (used as an information source for other students).
7. Links to fee-based Web information sources (such as *Ebsco Magazine* index, Gale Research databases, Sirs Researcher, etc.) and the online catalog.
8. Guidelines: AUPs, style sheets, copyright information, evaluation form.
9. Searching: Tips and strategies, listing of directories and search engines, and KidsConnect.
10. Teachers' Professional Resources: Links to lesson plans, national standards, restructuring schools, technology integration strategies and resources, information literacy, and AskERIC.
11. Links to departments, school, and district pages, local colleges, local public libraries, community resources, and other school libraries.
12. Links to information about books and reading on the Web.
13. Library-produced materials (instructional guides, curriculum units, etc.).
14. Links to Web sites for parents; family-related sites.

Remember that quality is more important than quantity. Developing a library home page is a dynamic process that constantly continues. Users will look forward to new additions. The box contains a listing of suggested content. The content of your library home page will depend on the needs of your school.

Curriculum Resource Guides

One of the most valuable sections of a school library home page is the curriculum resource guide, an evaluated, annotated listing of Web sites that support or enhance the curriculum. The guide transforms the Internet into a valuable information environment for students and faculty. The resource guide directs users through a maze of information by identifying and describing resources with valuable content, reducing the amount of time students and teachers spend sifting through layers of information before they find what they need. A resource guide helps keep students focused on relevant information and content and reduces the chances of getting sidetracked. School librarians' experience with organizing information and producing pathfinders to information topics, coupled with their knowledge of curriculum, makes them ideal developers of Web-based guides to Internet resources.

Writing annotations for each Web site listed in the resource guide can be time-consuming, but the added value is enormous. Often the Web site's title is not enough to indicate whether the information a student or faculty member needs is contained on that home page. A few concise, evaluative sentences describing the contents of the site is a tremendous help in guiding users to appropriate resources. Chico High School Library home page's curriculum links are well annotated by librarian Peter Milbury at http://www.cusd.chico.k12.ca.us/~pmilbury/lib.html. (See Figure 7.1.)

There are different approaches to organizing the Web sites in the resource guide. A majority of school libraries divide the Web sites by curriculum or special topics. Mt. Laurel

Figure 7.1
Carefully annotated Web site listings are an invaluable help for users. This home page of the Chico High School library is a good example of useful annotations.

Hartford School's Library Without Walls home page uses the Dewey Decimal Classification System at http://www.voicenet.com /~srussell/student.html. (See Figure 7.2.)

From there, click on the hot link for suggestions on where to find various topics classified by the Dewey Decimal System. (See Figure 7.3.)

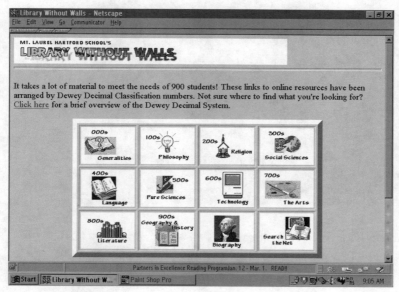

Figure 7.2
Another way to classify information is shown here on the Library Without Walls home page from Mt. Laurel Hartford School.

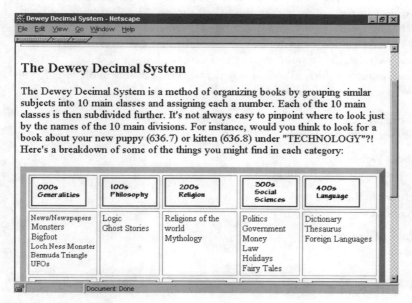

Figure 7.3
By drilling down, you can find Dewey Decimal classifications for the information you're seeking.

Figure 7.4
Another approach to information classification is the topic approach,
as shown by the home page of the Faircrest Memorial Middle School library.

Faircrest Memorial Middle School in Ohio uses a topic approach with a table format. Find their web page at http://jasper.stark.k12.oh.us/library/menu6.html. (See Figure 7.4.)

It's not necessary to start from scratch in developing the library home page resource guide. Look at a few of the established Internet resource guides (such as the Busy Teacher's Web site or the Argus Clearinghouse) and examine their choices. The most important consideration for including a Web site in your resource guide is whether it supports the school's curriculum. The resource guide should not be a listing of the best Web sites on the Internet, but rather the best Web sites that support your school's curriculum.

Start with these resource guides, as well as others mentioned in this book, to help you identify quality Web sites that are relevant to your school's curriculum.

Argus Clearinghouse
http://www.clearinghouse.net/

Busy Teacher's Web Site
http://www.ceismc.gatech.edu/busyt/

Jenny's Cybrary to the Stars
http://sashimi.wwa.com/~jayhawk/

Internet Public Library
http://www.ipl.org/

LION, information resources for K–12 school librarians
   http://www.libertynet.org/~lion/lion.html

School Librarians Links
   http://www.yab.com:80/~cyberian

Teachers Helping Teachers
   http://www.pacificnet.net/~mendel

Where the Wild Things Are: Librarian's Guide to the Best Information on the Net
   http://www.sau.edu/CWIS/Internet/wild/index.htm

700+ Great Sites
   http://www.ala.org/parentspage/greatsites

ICONNECT
Need help in developing a library home page? Sign up for a free online course on the ICONnect Web site. Learn about page design, layout, content, and more.

Add Special Lists to Web Sites for Faculty

In addition to Web sites for each curriculum area, some library pages have identified Web sites for use by specific teachers or classes. These Web sites are usually very targeted and narrow in content, and are generally not used by the school population. One example might be Web sites on fractal mathematics for a math teacher. The listing of these special topic Web sites can be added or removed from the library home page as teachers need them. This is similar to putting books on reserve for a limited amount of time.

Create Original Content

Although one of the primary purposes of the library home page is to help students and teachers select Web sites that support their curriculum and information needs, don't underestimate the significance of content. The library home page will be more valuable and useful if it contains original content, written by the school librarian, teachers, or students.

The library home page in Delaware's Newark Memorial High School offers an Internet Tour for students, complete with a test, at http://www.infolane.com/nm-library/itblcon.html. (See Figure 7.5.)

Frances Jacobson, school librarian at University High School in Illinois, along with Barbara Wysocki, a history teacher, developed an interdisciplinary curriculum unit in the American Memory Fellows Program. "Learning About Immigration Through Oral History" is available on the University High School Library home page at http://www.uni.uiuc.edu/library/ammem.html. (See Figure 7.6.)

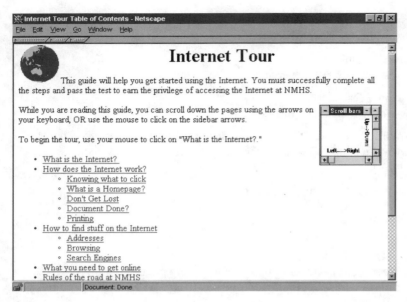

Figure 7.5
Pay attention to the content of your library home page. This site from
Newark Memorial High School offers an Internet tour.

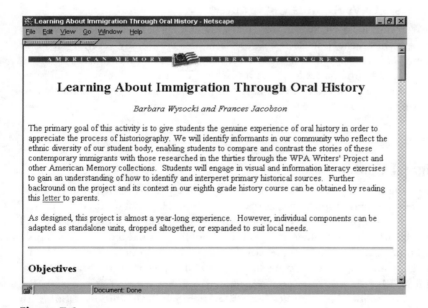

Figure 7.6
More content-related Web sites can be found at the Learning About Immigration
Through Oral History pages from University High School.

Debbie Abilock, the Library Media Teacher at Nueva Center for Learning in Hillsborough, California, designed a "search engine," a guide to help students choose the best search engine. A growing number of school library home pages are linking to the Nueva

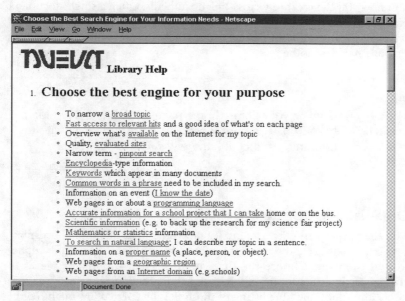

Figure 7.7
The Nueva Center for Learning has a search engine to find the best
search engines!

library home page to access this helpful tool. Logon to http://www.nueva.pvt.k12.ca.
us/~debbie/library/research/adviceengine.html. (See Figure 7.7.)

Announcing New Information on the Home Page

It's important to let the students and teachers know when you have added or changed
information on the Web site. Many Web sites have a section such as "what's new and different" and update it as often as possible, maybe every two weeks or so. Some school
libraries temporarily add information to this section, such as announcement of new books
or additional Web sites added to the resource guide. A topical listing of Web sites (such as
Black History Month or Banned Books Week) could also be highlighted in this section. Put
an announcement in the morning bulletin to draw attention to the library Web site or ask
a student to write an article about the library Web site for the school newspaper. Use an
eye-catching graphic on the home page, like **New** or **Hot News** and link it to the current
information. Users will have easy access to the information by clicking on the graphic.

ORGANIZE AND DESIGN THE LIBRARY HOME PAGE

Gather the Documents for Your Content

Collect all the policies, guidelines, forms, and documents you plan to incorporate into your
library home page. Start to write the content that is needed. Identify, evaluate, and annotate
Web sites to include in the curriculum areas. Keep these files in a folder on your own hard
disk as you organize yourself. Think carefully about how your documents can link to each

other. Think about how you can creatively cross-link documents. Often a single document will refer to several documents. Each of those references can be an active link to a document or to specific parts of documents. Use the linking feature of hypertext to link documents in addition to linking one page to another.

TIP
Make documents on your library home page available to download through Adobe Acrobat Capture. Logon to the Adobe Web site to learn more about this product at http://www.adobe.com.

Choose an Organizational Structure

Having decided on the purpose and the content, it's now time to decide on the organizational structure. It's important to choose an organizational theme that supports and emphasizes the purpose of the page. Choose the three or four most important pieces of information and organize the structure around them. If helping students have easy access to relevant Web sites is important, then the listing of those sites by curriculum might be the focus of the page. Some pages emphasize links to resources and divide the home page by resources available for specific users, student resources, teacher resources, and parent resources. The varied ways school librarians have chosen to organize the information on their home pages is as different as the physical layout of individual school libraries. Stetson Middle School Library, Virtual Branch maintained by Lynn Bertland in Philadelphia, has divisions and sub-categories. Logon to http://www.voicenet.com/~bertland/index.html. (See Figure 7.8.)

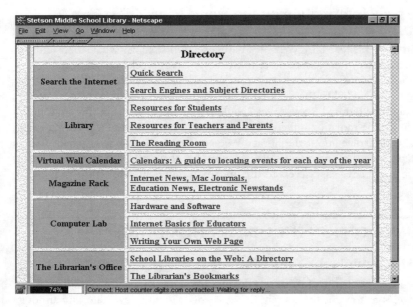

Figure 7.8
Stetson Middle School Library, Virtual Branch, has six major divisions and subcategories.

Myra Simons, librarian at the Georgia O'Keeffe Elementary School in Albuquerque, New Mexico, organizes the home page with an image map and a tabbed book. Logon to http://okeeffe.aps.edu/Okeeffe_Web/ Library/default.html. (See Figure 7.9.)

Librarian Alicia M. Astorga of Ursuline Academy in Delaware uses frames to focus on Internet searching on the right and listing of subject-related Web sites on the left. Logon at http://www.ursuline.org/library/text.htm. (See Figure 7.10.)

Figure 7.9
The home page of the Georgia O'Keeffe Elementary School is organized with an image map of a tabbed book.

Frances D. Aley, school librarian at Boothbay Region High School in Boothbay Harbor, Maine, focuses on golden retrievers as a central theme. Logon to http://www.biddeford.com/brhs/ to see a delightful page emphasizing a local interest. (See Figure 7.11.)

Whatever you choose, organize the page so that a user knows immediately what is important and has direct access to it. Decide how your Web pages will relate to each other and begin to "storyboard" your Web structure to get a detailed picture of the organization. Make sure your organizational structure is balanced and the important information your users want is not too deeply buried in the Web site. As you storyboard, check that the structure is not too shallow with a large number of menus on one level with no depth of content. The opposite structure, too deep, with too much vertical information, leaves the information buried beneath layers of menus. (See Figure 7.12.)

Develop an Overall Look

Decide on what graphic or text elements are common to each page, such as school or library logos, title, lines, menu bars, navigation buttons, author information, copyright statement,

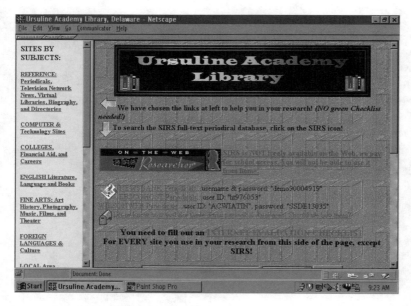

Figure 7.10
The Ursuline Academy library home page contains online subscriptions
on one side and subject-related Web sites on the other.

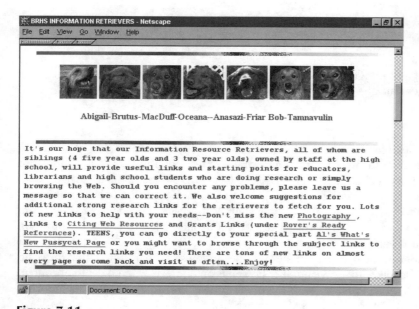

Figure 7.11
Another way to organize a home page is to choose a central theme.
This page from the Boothbay Region High School library uses
Golden Retrievers.

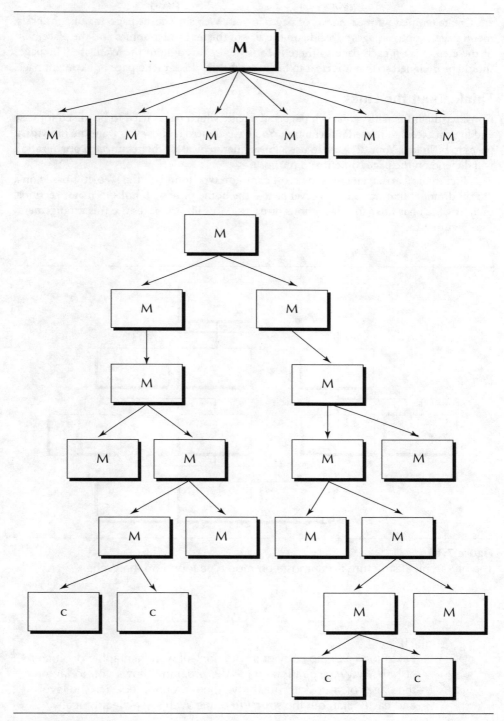

Figure 7.12
Examples of two structures to avoid. The first example is too shallow; the second is too deep.

etc. Create templates for each level of pages in your Web site (home page, major sub-levels, menu pages, content pages). Decide on the size of the text and graphics and the placement of the elements on each page so there is consistency throughout the Web site. The pages should be designed so that it is clear to the user whether it is a menu page or a content page.

Think about the Links

Consider the information on each page and decide which pages need to be linked for easy and logical access to related information. You have choices on how you want the individual pages to be linked. Your decision to use a linear, hierarchical, or interconnected organization will depend on the page content and purpose.

A hierarchical arrangement is the most common type found on the Web. It is based on a pyramid model that has one top-level page—the home page with links to major sections, each of which has links to sub-sections or pages. Most library pages use this arrangement. (See Figure 7.13.)

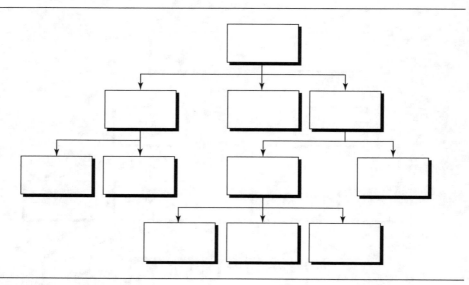

Figure 7.13
The hierarchical structure is the most common type found on the Web.

TIP
Download a demo copy of Inspiration software, a graphic organizer at http://www.inspiration.com. The program allows you to lay out the pages of your Web site, move them around, redesign the levels, and easily plan out the structure of the Web site—electronically.

A linear arrangement is helpful with pages that are directed to students and that you want to be sure are seen in the sequence you have established. Without any other choice to link, students must follow the prescribed linear path, such as Web pages explaining how to use search engines. (See Figure 7.14.)

The interconnected type of Web page arrangement assumes that there is no one page to start your discovery. Every page is connected to every other page. Users move through the Web site finding information based on their needs. This type of arrangement would be useful with a sub-set of pages, such as ones that contain links to external Web sites that support the curriculum. Students could easily jump among the listings of curriculum-based Web sites. (See Figure 7.15.)

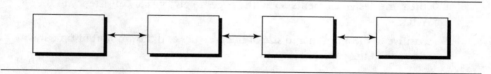

Figure 7.14
If viewing the pages in a certain order is important, then a linear structure may be the best for a section of your Web site.

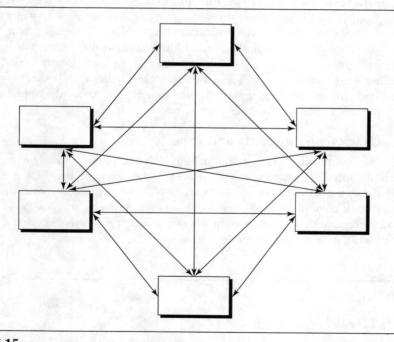

Figure 7.15
The interconnected structure of web pages allows users to jump freely from one site to another and all around.

Consider Some Web Design Guidelines

Keep sentences simple and to the point and use the active voice.

Use headlines rather than blocks of text when possible.

Use bold or italic to set text apart, rather than all capital letters.

Use bulleted information.

Place important text in a border.

Use only one type of line and be consistent through the Web site.

Icons should clearly represent what they are intended to.

Pictures must be relevant to the text.

Use dark text on a light background, never the opposite.

Use the same design elements on all the pages to give visual consistency to the Web site.

Be sensitive to the amount and size of the graphics and the amount of time it will take to load the page.

Interactivity

The power of the Internet lies in its ability to allow people to interact, to share, and to contribute. Whenever possible, capitalize on this feature. Use an e-mail form for users to contribute suggestions on improving the library Web site. Encourage students and faculty to suggest sites to be added to the resources guide. A public library in Massachusetts (http://www.netcaster.com/rpl/booktop.html) has forms on one of its Web pages that patrons can use to submit book reviews. You can also search the site for reviews. If this were to be implemented on a school library home page, it would give students a wider audience for their book reviews and offer peer guidance in choosing books to read. Libraries Forms List (http://hertz.njit.edu/~robertso/LibForms.html) provides a list of library Web sites that offer forms for interlibrary loan and document delivery requests, reference question submissions, literature search requests, acquisition recommendations, and other types of customer feedback. Most links are to universities and colleges, but it provides a good sampling of what is possible to provide on library Web sites.

Get Feedback from Students and Faculty

As soon as you put together the first draft of your Web site, show it to students and faculty for their input. Ask them what the first things are that they see when they look at each page. Ask them if they think the graphic elements are helpful in navigating the Web site. Do they like the choice of color, the use of lines? Based on their feedback, go back to the drawing board and implement the suggestions. The Web site will always be dynamic, changing as the technology and your users' needs change.

AUTHORING

What Is HTML?

Hypertext mark-up language (HTML) is the basic language of the World Wide Web. It is a system for marking up documents with informational tags that indicates how text in the documents should be presented and how the documents are linked together. Basic HTML is simple and can be mastered by you, your staff, or student assistants.

HTML tags consist of a left angle bracket "<" (a "less than" symbol) followed by the name of the tag. It is closed by a right angle bracket ">" (a "greater than" symbol). Tags are paired, with the end tag looking like the beginning tag except a "/" (slash sign) precedes the text within the two brackets. All HTML documents start with <HTML> and end with <HTML>. Between those codes are two sections, the head and the body. They are marked at the start and the end as <HEAD> <HEAD> and <BODY> <BODY>. Notice the slash "/" denotes the end of the head and body. A minimal HTML document using a few basic tags looks like this:

>   <HTML> here comes the HTML document
>
>   <HEAD> this is the beginning of the head
>
>   </HEAD> this is the end of the head
>
>   <BODY> this is the beginning of the body
>
>   </BODY> this is the end of the body
>
>   </HTML> this is the end of the HTML document

The HTML code of a simple library home page would look like this:

>   <HTML>
>
>   <HEAD><TITLE>Anywhere School Library</TITLE> </HEAD>
>
>   <H1><CENTER>Anywhere School Library</CENTER></H1>
>
>   <H2><CENTER>Virtual Branch</CENTER></H2>
>
>   <P>

The body of the text is placed here. It could include a brief introductory statement about the virtual library, its purpose, and its objectives.

>   <P>

Listed below could be hotlinks to the various sections of the virtual library home page, such as a resource guide of relevant Web sites, searching tips and strategies, and a special section for teachers and parents.

>   <H3><CENTER>Resource Guide Searching Tips & Strategies Parent Resources
>   Teacher Resources</CENTER></H3>
>
>   </BODY>
>
>   </HTML>

And the page would look as shown in Figure 7.16.

In most browsers it's easy to take a look at the underlying HTML document that's the source for the displayed page. In Netscape, choose View, then Document Source. The HTML source document will appear in a new window. You can select and copy the sample HTML from a window and paste it into a file. Looking at HTML code for interesting pages is a good way to learn HTML. (See Figure 7.17.)

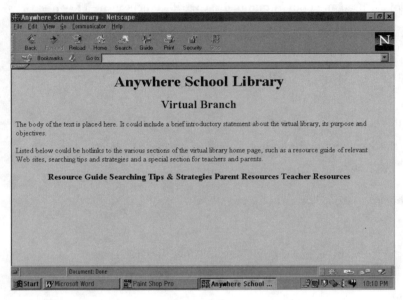

Figure 7.16
A sample library home page for you to follow.

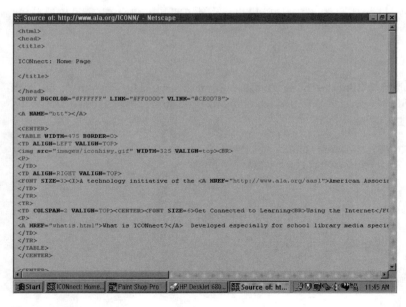

Figure 7.17
Sample view source code in Netscape.

HTML Editing Programs

You can program your library Web page in several ways. One way is by manually using HTML code. Another is by using stand alone editor programs that automatically generate HTML code. Add-on packages for various word processing programs can also create the special code. Since school librarians are always pressed for time, I would recommend using a WYSIWYG ("What You See Is What You Get") editor that makes it easy for beginners to create home pages. Following are five of the most well known HTML editors. These are not the only ones on the market, however.

> Microsoft Front Page
>   http://www.microsoft.com/frontpage
>
> Netscape Navigator Gold
>   http://home.netscape.com/comprod/
>
> Adobe Pagemill
>   http://www.adobe.com
>
> Sunburst's Web Workshop
>   http://www.sunburst.com
>
> Claris Home Page
>   http://www.claris.com/index.html

There are also freeware editors (offered by publishers at no cost) and shareware editors (you try it out at no cost and if you like it, then send in the money). Two of these are: HoTMedal for Windows at http://www.sq.com/ and HotDog at http://www.sausage.com/. If you want more of these products, go to Mag's Big List of HTML Editors at http://www.hypernews.org/HyperNews/get/www/html/editors.html.

TIP
If your school doesn't have a Web server, then visit the Global School House Web site. They offer free space on their file servers to mount school Web sites. Find out more information at http://www.gsh.org.

Web Development Support for Educators

Web66 at http://web66.coled.umn.edu features one of the oldest and most comprehensive "registries" of K–12 schools on the Web. In addition, it offers "share pages" with helpful HTML examples you can download for your own use.

Global Schoolhouse at http://www.gsh.org, founded by Global SchoolNet Foundation and sponsored by Microsoft, offers free space to any school that wants to put up a home page but doesn't have a server or a local Internet Service Provider. And Classroom Connect at http://www.classroom.net/ offers online forms to help you launch a Web site.

School Web Page Development Guide

http://www.massnetworks.org/~nicoley/schools/

Guidelines for creating school pages, clipart, and templates.

Creating Web Pages for K–12 Schools and Libraries

http://www.libertynet.org/~lion/web-pages.html

Contains resources useful to librarians, teachers, students, and others involved in creating and managing Web pages for K–12 schools and libraries.

Library Web Manager's Reference Guide

http://sunsite.berkeley.edu/Web4Lib/index.html

Includes hot topics from the Web4Lib listserv.

For more Web sites on web development and support, understanding HTML, and clip art for library home pages, see appendix D.

LAUNCHING YOUR LIBRARY HOME PAGE

Once you have developed and tested your Web site, you need to let students, faculty, administrators and parents know about your page. Use all the regular vehicles for communication in the school community. Encourage students to write up an article for the school newspaper, ask the PTA to include a notice in their newsletters or other communications to parents, include it in the morning announcements, design a flyer for the school bulletin boards announcing the library Web site, and make a presentation at a staff meeting explaining how the library home page supports teaching and learning. In addition you will want to send an e-mail to Peter Milbury (http://www.cusd.chico.k12.ca.us /~pmilbury/lib.html and Linda Bertland (http://www.voicenet.com/~bertland/index.html) to have your page included in their directories of school library Web sites. You can find their e-mail addresses on their home pages. You might also want to send an announcement to LM_NET, the school librarians' listserv, to let your colleagues know you have launched a Web site.

ADVANCED STRATEGY
Include an interactive form on your library home page for students and teachers to ask you for help in locating information. You can archive the questions and answers and develop a school library FAQ.

Consider an Internal Home Page

If you do not have the capability to launch your school library home page on the Internet (or perhaps your school district is not yet ready), you can still use it internally by loading the library home page on the PC's hard drive. You do not need a bank of computers and a high-speed communications line to use a library home page effectively. There are different levels of publishing. If your library has one computer hooked up to the Internet with a modem and a phone line, you can use a library home page by loading it on your computer's hard drive. When the browser comes up, the library home page will appear. Users sitting at that computer will have access to the home page. Since it is not mounted on a file server, it is not accessible to anyone on the Internet, just those sitting at that computer. In this way you are assisting students and faculty in navigating the Web, customizing what they see first as they logon.

It's an easy process to do. When you start up your Internet browser, it automatically links to a site on the Web. This is called the default home page and is usually the Web site of the company that developed the browser. Netscape links you to its home page at http://home.netscape.com. Microsoft links you to its home page at http://home.microsoft.com. You can reset the default page in Netscape by selecting Edit, then Preferences. Reset the preference by typing in a new path statement in the Home Page Location box. The path statement should begin with the word "file" followed by a colon, three forward slashes, the letter "C", the pipe (|) character, another forward slash and the name of the directory where the home page is stored. The full path statement will look like this: file:///C|/Library/index.html. When you are finished, click on OK to save your setting. The next time you open the browser, the library home page will appear. If there is a local area network in the building, this file can be saved in a shared directory so everyone on the network will have access to it, though it will still not be accessible to anyone outside the school network. This is a good way to first launch your library home page. You can ask for feedback from faculty and students before you go online to the world.

Chapter 8

Teaching the Internet

School librarians have a unique opportunity to take a leadership role in introducing and teaching the faculty, administrators, and parents about the Internet. School district staff is becoming more and more involved in seeking and taking advantage of opportunities to improve their professional skills and increase their effectiveness in using technology. School librarians, with their knowledge of and experience with information systems, the information search process, teaching, and curriculum are in a pivotal position to offer support, guidance, and staff development.

The Internet is a great information resource; however, it is often confusing and frustrating to use even though it appears easily accessible. Often, teachers and parents find it overwhelming. All the information is there, just a point and click away, but the right information is hard to find. And when you do locate the information, you need to critically evaluate it. Instruction is needed to successfully navigate the Internet, use search engines and directories, and evaluate Web sites. Teachers need additional help in integrating the Internet into the curriculum in meaningful and relevant ways. Parents need guidance in working with children at home on the Internet.

The Internet is available everywhere—at home, in the office, in the classroom, even at coffeehouses and shopping malls. As more and more schools install computer networks with workstations in the classrooms, kids will be accessing the online catalog, subject-specialized CD-ROMs, and the Internet from there. The "school library without walls" is an environment where information is delivered to the student and teacher in the classroom to support and be integrated into the teaching and learning process. This places an increased responsibility on the classroom teacher to be able to assist students in the information research process. Since they are no longer physically in the library to conduct all their research, the school librarian is less likely to be available to assist them. In this new scenario, students turn to their classroom teachers for assistance. At home, they turn to their parents. This shifts the focus from working only with students to increased staff development opportunities with teachers and support and guidance to parents.

The Internet is changing how libraries deliver services. It forces school librarians to re-examine the role the school library plays in the teaching and learning process and encourages them to expand their vision to include new programs and solutions. The Internet allows school librarians to collaborate with parents and teachers by developing public relations strategies to reach out to parents and staff development programs to support teachers. Through these strategies, the school library will remain the information center of the school.

TEACHING THE FACULTY

There are many different strategies, both in-house and online, that you can use to teach the faculty to use the Internet effectively. You can develop workshops, modify existing courses, point them to online courses on the Internet, or run informal lunchtime sessions. As you work on these new strategies, don't ignore the possibilities for communication and instruction through the existing school structure such as staff meetings; articles, columns, and notices in school and district newsletters; memos; e-mail; and notices to faculty.

Adult Learning Theories

Whatever strategies you decide to implement, first read some of the latest research on adult learners and staff development. Theresa E. Kirkpatrick of Indiana State University Library has put together Adult Learning Theory: A Resource Guide, at http://odin.indstate.edu/level1.dir/adultlrn.html. It divides the literature of the field into five sections: General, Andragogy, Self-Directed Learning, Transformational Learning, and Adult Learning Theory in a Variety of Environments, and includes Journals and Resource Organizations. Another good source is Staff Development by Jocelyn Butler at http://www.nwrel.org/scpd/sirs/6/cu12.html. It is part of the School Improvement Research Series and focuses on three areas of effective staff development: (1) needs and characteristics of participant learners, (2) the program characteristics of purposes, structure, content, process and follow-up, and (3) the organizational characteristics that contribute to effective staff development.

TEACHING THE INTERNET

How do you teach the Internet using the Internet? Learn about Web sites that will help students, teachers, and parents navigate and use the Web. Take a CyberTour to visit exemplary Web sites that teach about the functions and special features of the Web.

Margaret Fryatt (http://www.oise.on.ca/~mfryatt/training/models.htm) presents Proposed Models for Successful Internet Implementation as part of Helping Teachers Find the On-Ramp to the Information Highway: Meeting the Challenges of Implementation and Training. Fryatt lists the advantages and disadvantages of various staff development strategies: outcome-based staff development, invitational immersion, providing "free" or "cheap" Internet access, and the cohort model. She also includes discussion on models for telecomputing training.

Develop Internet Workshops

The first step in designing instruction is to find out what the learners need to know. This can be done through a faculty survey or needs assessment, by conducting focus groups, or by talking to department chairs. With this information, workshops for different levels can be developed. The most effective way to learn about the Internet is hands-on exploration of the procedures demonstrated. Follow-up practice questions on specific curriculum areas reinforce teacher motivation by focusing on the value of the Internet to their teaching. Training results are better if the training can be broken down into small sections or topics and spread over an extended period of time. This allows the learner more time to practice the skills that they are trying to learn, creates more opportunities for collaborative work, and allows time for independent exploration.

In general, the beginning Internet workshop needs to address.[1]

1. What the Internet is
2. A brief history
3. How to connect to the Internet
4. What kinds of resources can be found on the Internet
5. Protocols of the Internet
    telnet
    gopher
    FTP
    World Wide Web
6. Functions of the Internet
    e-mail—how to send e-mail
    listserv—how to locate listservs and sign up
    chat—how to join and use chat
    Usenet—how to join a newsgroup
7. How to navigate a WWW browser
8. Guided practice with demonstration sites

ICONnect
For copies of handouts for the Internet Workshop described in this chapter (List of Web sites and Internet Glossary), check the ICONnect online course, The School Library Media Specialist of the 21st Century, archive.

Intermediate learners are ready to learn how to locate, evaluate, and manage Internet resources.[2]

A.   Using search engines effectively
    1. Search engines and directories
    2. Differences between the two
    3. Strategies for using search engines effectively
B.   How to evaluate Web sites
    1. Areas to evaluate: authority, content, technical aspects, design, navigation, curriculum connections, and learning environment
    2. Evaluation forms
    3. Teaching students to evaluate Web sites
    4. Recommended sites for evaluation forms, hand-outs, and presentations
C.   How to manage Internet resources
    1. Organizing, saving, importing, and opening bookmark files
    2. Downloading files: programs, graphics, plug-ins, and helper applications
    3. Using multiple applications simultaneously and managing your desktop

Additional workshops can be developed for users concentrating on topics and issues important to K–12 education such as student access and acceptable use policies, filters, and censorship; HTML and developing home pages; copyright and fair use; safety and supervision; and accessing information for specific curriculum areas or topics.

Offer Online Courses

The American Association of School Librarians' ICONnect offers an excellent opportunity for school librarians to deliver online Internet training to their faculty. ICONnect has developed a series of online courses written specifically for K–12 librarians and educators. AASL makes these courses available to school librarians and other educators to re-package and offer to their faculty, administrators, district librarians, and parents. The only requirement is that you give credit to the American Association of School Librarians and the ICONnect Task Force, including the URL http://www.ala.org/ICONN.

The courses are on a wide range of topics, all pertinent to the integration of the Internet into the curriculum. They include the following. (See Figure 8.1.)

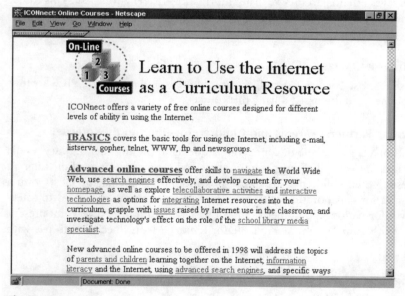

Figure 8.1
ICONnect, from the American Association of School Librarians, offers online courses on Internet training.

IBASICS—Internet Basics

An introductory level course focusing on Internet basics and designed for school library media specialists who have basic knowledge of e-mail and an Internet e-mail connection. IBASICS covers basic tools for using the Internet, including e-mail, listservs, gopher, telnet, WWW, ftp, and newsgroups. Curriculum threads are woven into each of these areas. Examples of how the Internet can be used in collaborative curriculum projects is also included in the lessons.

CurriWeb—Curriculum Integration Using the Web

Curriculum Integration is one of the key factors in the success or failure of any new development in education. If it doesn't work in the classroom and help the students learn, why use it? This course covers the whys and the hows of using Internet and Web-related material in the classroom, and how to make it successful.

ElemCurr—Integrating the Internet into the Elementary Curriculum

This course focuses on four themes for use with elementary-age students to help teachers and information specialists build cross-disciplinary lessons incorporating the Internet.

HomePage—Developing Content for Your Home Page

The content of a Home Page is as important as its design. Learn about design, layout, and content as a Home Page is constructed.

InformLit—Information Literacy and the Internet

Information literacy is essential to survive in an information-rich environment. This course explores the technology skills needed to effectively locate, access, and use information on the Internet.

Issues—K–12 Internet Issues

Copyright, Acceptable Use Policies, Citing Electronic Sources, and Filters and PICS are four of the issues explained and discussed during this course.

Partners—Learning Partners: Parents and Children Together on the Internet

Now that schools play a major role in connecting students to the Internet, Library Media Specialists must take the lead in helping parents understand the many aspects of the Internet and its usefulness to their children. This course provides library media specialists with a toolkit of resources for collaboration with parents. Particular attention is paid to safety issues, parenting information, and homework resources. In addition, a PowerPoint presentation, "Log On With Your Family," is available for Library Media Specialists to use with parent groups.

SearchE—Using Internet and Web Search Engines Effectively

This course helps media specialists and educators find information on the Internet using search engines. Some advanced search features are explained and investigated, and practical tips are presented in each session. Meta search engines, how they work, and how to get good results, working knowledge of Boolean logic, and what tools work best in which situations is explored.

SLMS21st—The School Library Media Specialist in the 21st Century

This course helps clarify and redefine the role of the school library media specialist for the twenty-first century. As technology is integrated into the curriculum on more and more levels, the SLMS will be taking a leadership role in building district staff development programs, as well as classroom/curriculum integration.

Teleco—Telecollaborative Activities on the 'Net

After completing this course, media specialists and classroom teachers will be more aware of the teaching/learning potential of telecollaborative projects; they learn how to set up effective projects, and how to locate, evaluate, and join existing telecollaborative projects.

Trends—New Trends in Interactivity on the Web

As fast as you can learn the latest technology, something else comes along to replace it. This course gives you a head start on the newest and latest interactive technologies for schools and education, including (but not limited to) HTML, Java, ActiveX, plug-ins, 3-D, and Virtual Reality.

WebNav—Navigating the World Wide Web

Find out why the Internet and the World Wide Web are so important for schools today. Examine their relevance to the students, to the curriculum, and to the jobs of school library media specialists.

These archived courses can be found at http://www.ala.org/ICONN/. Librarians can download the courses and modify them to meet the unique needs of their district, including e-mail instructions and individuals to contact for more help. The courses can be distributed through a listserv, if your district has the capacity, or by setting up a group distribution list in e-mail. Each course consists of four lessons so participants would receive one lesson each week for four weeks. Districts could combine the online course with other Internet functions to increase collaboration among participants, such as a listserv, a chat room, or a newsgroup open only to the participants of the course. The only requirement is that credit be given to the American Association of School Librarians. A statement should be included with each lesson along with the Web address of the ICONnect Web site. Additional information can be found on the ICONnect Web site at http://www.ala.org/ICONN.

Your district, with the addition of an assessment, could offer in-service credit for the online courses. When Byram Hills Central School District in Armonk, New York, offered some of the ICONnect online courses for in-service credit, they developed project-based assessments. For the course on effective use of search engines, the assessment was:

> In a collaborative group of 3–4, teachers develop an Internet-based, curriculum project using essential questions. Include activities to purposefully give students experience in learning how to effectively use search engines and directories. Include objectives, a time line and structure, Web resources, and a method of evaluating students.

Upon completion of an online course and the assessment project, teachers received one in-service credit, based on 15 hours of work. The curriculum units can be shared with the rest of the staff on the district Web site.

 TIP
Use a library bulletin board for "Challenging Searches"—difficult Internet searches, questions, or topics faculty or students couldn't find information on. Challenge others to collaborate, use new approaches, and post the strategy they used and the results they found.

If you want to package online courses you have developed, these sites will help you get started.

Learning on the Web: An Instructor's Manual

> http://teleeducation.nb.ca/lotw/
>
> This manual helps instructors adapt and develop their courses for delivery using the Web.

Delivering Instruction on the World Wide Web

> http://ccwf.cc.utexas.edu/~mcmanus/wbi.html
>
> Explains some of the basic issues involved in Web-based instruction.

NICENET's Internet Classroom Assistant

> http://www.nicenet.net/ica/ica_info.cfm
>
> A free Web-based conferencing, personal messaging, document sharing, scheduling, and link/resource sharing tool. Open to all secondary and post-secondary educators to use.

ICONnect

Logon to the ICONnect Web site and sign up for the free online course, The Library Media Specialist in the 21st Century. Learn how to assume the leadership role in building and district staff development programs, as well as classroom/curriculum integration.

Publicize Internet Online Courses

There are many Internet courses offered for free. Although most are general "how-to" courses that are not specialized for educators, they are worthwhile to take and can provide an understanding of the Internet and its functions. It would be helpful to faculty to provide a listing of these courses on a continual basis, updating the information as necessary. The library home page would be an excellent location, providing easy access for everyone. Following is a sampling of the types of Web sites delivering tutorials to learn about the Internet. To learn about additional tutorials, go to Yahoo, Internet Beginner's Guide and World Wide Web Beginner's Guide.

Scout Report Signpost

> http://www.signpost.org/signpost/
>
> "Contains only the best Internet resources, as chosen by the staff of the Scout Report, cataloged and organized for efficient browsing and searching." Do a Quick Search with the keyword *Internet* for a listing of courses on how to use the Internet.

BCK2SKOL

> http://www.sc.edu/bck2skol/
>
> This well-designed site presents a beginner's course on the Net and its various tools targeted toward librarians and other information professionals. Lessons include information on participating in mailing lists and usenet newgroups, and they cover basic Internet tools including telnet, FTP, archie, gopher, veronica, and the World Wide Web. In addition, the class provides pointers to librarians on researching the Net in eight different academic subject areas. (See Figure 8.2.)

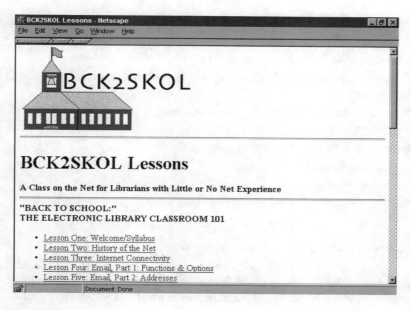

Figure 8.2
The BCK2SKOL Web site offers beginning courses on learning to use
the Internet.

Internet Tour—Newark Memorial High School's Tutorial on the Internet

http://www.infolane.com/nm-library/itblcon.html

This guide is designed for high school students, but it is excellent for Internet
beginners of all ages to help get started using the Internet. It includes: What is the
Internet? How does the Internet work? Knowing what to click, What is a
Homepage? Don't Get Lost, Document Done? Printing, How to find stuff on the
Internet, Addresses, Browsing, Search Engines, What you need to get on-line, and
Pass the Test!

ADVANCED STRATEGY
Logon to Education World at http://www.education-world.com to get
a free copy of Net Lessons. Education World teamed up with O'Reilly
Publishing, Inc., to publish a 30-page booklet entitled, *Net Lessons:
Education World's Internet Primer.* This booklet, free to educators, featured ideas on how to integrate the Internet into the classroom, as well
as hands-on lesson plans to get teachers started.

Harnessing the Power of the Web

http://www.gsn.org/web/index.html

This tutorial shows K–12 teachers, step-by-step, how to harness this exciting
power of the World Wide Web for classroom use. It is "a concise (not comprehensive) collection of ideas, examples, resources, and tools which emphasizes
student project-based learning activities, Web publishing as a multimedia presentation tool, and communications on the Internet to foster peer and commu-

nity review and feedback. It is designed to help a teacher with limited or no experience with the Web to:

- Learn about the World Wide Web and how to use a Web browser
- Understand the unique role of the Internet as a communications and collaboration medium
- Design a student-centered project-based learning activity suitable for WWW presentation
- Design a classroom or personal home page
- Publish student work on the Web
- Develop and use strategies to develop dialog between author and audience, including formal and informal peer and community review and evaluation

WebHound

http://www.mcli.dist.maricopa.edu/webhound/index.html

An excellent introduction to Web searching in which, through a series of carefully designed steps, the WebHound introduces you to information, provides guided examples, and then sends you off for some hands-on practice. (See Figure 8.3.)

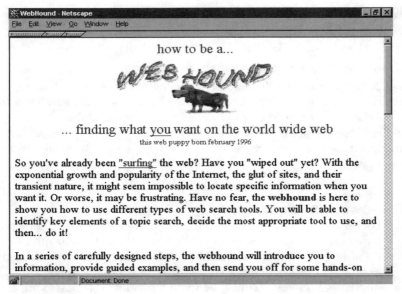

Figure 8.3
Learn how to search the World Wide Web by using this WebHound site.

CyberEd

http://www.umassed.edu/cybered/distlearninghome.html

These no-credit, fee-based courses on Web site development "use this new technology to try to: get away from the old classroom lecture model, and into the model of individual exploration, move the student out of the role of being a passive absorber of information and into the role of active apprentice where possible, encourage team work among students, as opposed to strictly individual assignments, use diverse tools, choosing those that best fit the individual situation at the time, help students to learn how to cope with rapidly changing information content." Rather than a self-directed online course, this one has set dates, a live instructor, other students, and lots of interaction.

Patrick Crispen's Internet Roadmap

http://www.brandonu.ca/~ennsnr/Resources/Roadmap/Welcome.html

Roadmap is a free Internet training workshop designed to teach new "Net travelers" how to travel around the rapidly expanding (and often confusing) "Information Superhighway" without getting lost. Using the latest information available coupled with guest lectures from some of today's most respected Internet leaders, Roadmap is one of the most talked-about Internet training workshops in history!

TIP

After you have taught workshop participants to effectively use search engines, get them involved in searching by challenging them with Internet Hunt questions at gopher://gopher.cic.net/1/hunt.

The Internet for Newbies

http://sen.wiu.edu/newbies/intronet.html

Maintained by the Central Illinois Adult Education Service Center College of Education and Human Services, Western Illinois University, this interactive page covers the basic information for beginning Internet navigation and searching.

Learn the Net

http://www.learnthenet.com/english/index.html

Includes a wide variety of courses including Getting Started, Internet Basics World Wide Web, E-mail, Newsgroups, Conferencing, Digging for Data, Doing Business, Web Publishing, Multimedia, and Glossary.com.

Learn the Internet

http://www.grandeprairie.org/newbies.html

Put together and maintained by the Virtual Grande Prairie Public Library, this site contains online courses such as E-mail, Usenet Newsgroups, The World Wide Web and Netscape, General Internet Help and Guides, Using and Understanding Search Engines, and Become a Webaholic—Get the Net at Home!

CyberU

http://dune.srhs.k12.nj.us/WWW/contents.htm

This site supports a one-semester, student-centered high school course that "introduces the Internet, what it is, and how to use its major applications." Includes resource links.

Internet Tutorials

http://www.albany.edu/library/internet/

Laura Cohen, a network librarian at the University at Albany, maintains this effective collection of beginner tutorials for Internet users. Under the five major categories of Basic Internet, Research Guides, Search Engines, Netscape, and Software Training, there are a total of 19 tutorials at present. They contain easily understandable advice on how to use and search the Internet. Some central elements include an excellent discussion of Boolean Searching (Venn diagrams included); a useful, concise discussion of evaluating Internet information; and four informative tutorials on search engines and subject directories.

WebTeacher

http://www.webteacher.org/winnet/index.html

An excellent site for beginners containing a series of short tutorials on basic Internet functions.

The Village from Global Village Communications

http://www.globalvillage.com/gcweb/tour.html

This Web site, directed to family or home use of the Internet, takes you on a tour of the Web where you will be checking the stock market, the latest news reports, researching a possible vendor and accounting software, hiring a new graphic designer, finding a government document, and sending birthday flowers. (See Figure 8.4.)

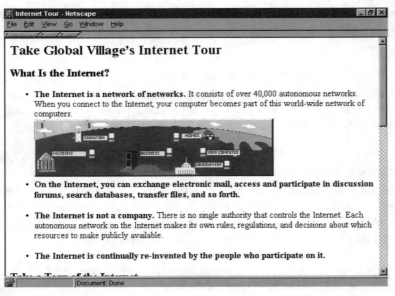

Figure 8.4
Take a tour of the Internet from the Global Village's Web site.

ACRL/CNI Internet Education Project

http://www.cwru.edu/affil/cni/base/goals.html

This project shows librarians how to display and share instructional materials that they have designed for teaching about seeking and evaluating information in a networked environment. The Project solicits Internet guides, syllabi, and other materials designed for user education. It reviews the methodology, content, organization, currency, and use of technology of submitted materials and shares those materials that receive excellent reviews.

"Brownbag" Training Sessions

"Brownbag" training sessions are popular with teachers because they are fun and less threatening than formal workshops, combining a social gathering with learning. These sessions usually last only one hour or so, sometimes longer, depending on the staff lunch periods in your school. It's a good time to entice the faculty with curriculum Web sites, present strategies to integrate the Internet into the curriculum, or offer practical tips for handling technology in the classroom. Concentrate on only one or two concepts per session and leave time for questions and answers. The topics of the sessions can be based on questions the library and technology staff receive from users and also on faculty requests for specific topics. Some suggested topics include:

Save Your Information to Drive A

Ports & Cables? Learn Where They Go

Find a File Using Windows Utility Program

Bookmark and Organize Your Favorite Web Sites

Set Up Pegasus Mail with Your Preferences

Understand Netscape Error Messages

Handle Common Printing Problems

Find KeyPals on the Internet

Outline Research and Take Notes—Electronically—with Research Assistant

Get Help on the Internet—KidsConnect Q&A Answer Service

Talk to Colleagues Around the Country—Join a Listserv

Find New Telecollaborative Projects on the Internet

Tips to Keep up with the Internet

Web Browsers . . . What Are They?

Downloading and Saving Graphic Files

The screen in Figure 8.5 shows the sample announcement of the CyberCafe, a "brownbag" session held for faculty and staff. A sample handout designed for participants is shown in Figure 8.6.

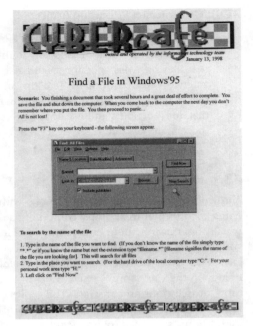

Figure 8.5
Get together with faculty and staff for a brownbag lunch. Make it a regular event to discuss different thoughts about or strategies for using the Internet.

Figure 8.6
Be sure to have hard copy handouts at your brownbag lunches so that participants can spend their time eating and listening rather than taking notes.

InterNIC and the Library and Information Technology Association (LITA), a division of the American Library Association (ALA), developed a series of 15 minute presentations on Internet topics. Each of the 15 Minute Series modules is structured as a mini-slide presentation and is designed to answer a specific Internet-related question. The first slide presents the answer to the question (What is . . . ? or How do I . . . ?). Subsequent slides develop the points in the outline, and the final slide summarizes the module's topic in narrative form. This series is excellent for "brownbag" sessions. They can be found at InterNIC 15-Minute Series http://rs.internic.net/nic-support/15min/intro.html. (See Figure 8.7.)

REACH OUT TO PARENTS

As students' use of the Internet in classrooms, libraries, and at home increases, so does the need to establish a closer relationship with parents. As partners in the education of their children, we need to have an open dialog with parents to discuss important issues such as access, safety, and copyright. Parents need to learn how to help their children become purposeful and thoughtful users of this vast information resource. In addition to articles, columns or notices in PTA newsletters, and presentations at PTA meetings, more outreach is needed. Some school libraries are starting to hold Family Technology Nights. Evening work-

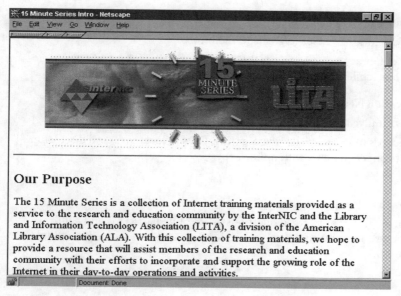

Figure 8.7
Do you have some short, specific questions about the Internet?
Try the 15 Minute Series modules for complete yet concise answers.

shops can be designed for parents to learn about the Internet, its functions, what is has to offer, strategies to use the Internet with their children, how to help kids use the Internet responsibly and for learning, and find out about good Web sites for kids and families.

ICONnect
A complete Family Technology Night powerpoint presentation is available on the ICONnect Web site as part of the free online course, Learning Partners: Parents and Children Together. You can download it from the archives and use it as it is designed or modify it to fit you needs.

There are many benefits for parents and children learning on the Internet together. The Internet offers access to interesting and fun Web sites to challenge and motivate them in all academic areas. It helps kids increase their technological skills and interact with kids around the world in a global community, building understanding and acceptance of other cultures. Finally, it provides an opportunity for parents and children to learn together and have fun. There are many Web sites to support family use of the Internet. Following are a few examples of Web sites that are helpful to parents and could be used as a handout at a family technology night. Or they could be made into a booklet of Web sites for parents. A full listing can be found in appendix C.

ICONnect
Logon to the ICONnect's Parents Page for more Web sites for families to investigate together, online courses to take, and links to explore.

50+ Great Sites for Kids and Parents

http://www.ala.org/parentspage/greatsites/50.html

An American Library Association site that includes top sites for preschool and elementary school children and their parents to explore together. (See Figure 8.8.)

The Family Education Network

http://www.familyeducation.com/

Offers hundreds of brief articles on parenting, links to local sites, and discussion boards that connect parents with online experts.

Parent Soup

http://www.parentsoup.com

Includes an archive of answers to questions asked of pediatricians and child development experts and advice about helping your children succeed in school. (See Figure 8.9.)

ICONnect

Point your browser to KidsConnect Favorite Web sites on the ICONNect Web site to see a list that KidsConnect volunteers have found to be the most helpful in answering kids' questions.

Figure 8.8

Get parents involved in using the Internet with their children. Try 50+ Great Sites from The Librarian's Guide to Cyberspace.

Figure 8.9
Parent Soup is a great site for parents looking for answers to common
questions about childhood.

IMPORTANT ISSUE: ACCEPTABLE USE POLICY

Teachers and parents are concerned about child safety issues on the Internet. Adults created
the Internet, and from the beginning it has contained adult material. As students become
computer-educated they have gained access to these materials which include sexually explic-
it images and text, information about drugs and violence, and programs to crash or disable
computer networks and systems. Educators and parents are concerned that students are
exposed to this age-inappropriate information. One method to educate and hold students
responsible for appropriate Internet usage is an Acceptable Use Policy (AUP).

The AUP, signed by students, parents, and faculty, outlines the acceptable and unacceptable uses of the online services in school. It helps protect students from inappropriate materials and the school from liability resulting from inappropriate student use of the Internet.
Developing a school-wide or district-wide Acceptable Use Policy can help students be aware
of and understand their responsibilities in using the Internet. Although AUPs are intended
to limit or remove liability of public schools from any misuse by students, they can also serve
a greater purpose by emphasizing the personal responsibility of students for their own
actions. When students are taught the rules of proper online behavior and are entrusted
with the opportunity to follow them, they gain decision-making skills and an increased
sense of responsibility.

ICONnect
Join the ICONnect free online course, K–12 Issues, to learn about
critical points that need to be addressed in an AUP.

The primary issues that need to be addressed in an acceptable use policy include the following.

1. *The purpose of the Internet access.* Discuss why you plan to offer Internet access to your students, stressing the value of the Internet as a school resource. Since many parents will not be familiar with educational uses of the Internet, include examples of curriculum-integrated projects.

2. *Types of information available and intellectual ownership.* Include a discussion of appropriate and inappropriate information that can be found, including objectionable material. Stress that Internet access is a privilege, not a right, and accessing objectionable material is a violation; explain the rules of copyright.

3. *User responsibilities.* Discuss the problem of limited resources, stressing the need to conserve bandwidth and respect other users' rights. Ethical issues, including unauthorized access, attempts to "crack" computer systems, lobbying, and illegal activities, need to be clearly stated.

4. *Personal security.* Students, especially those in the lower elementary grades, tend to be very trusting, even on the Internet, so they need to be cautioned. Remind students not to give out personal information such as last name, telephone number, or address.

5. *Penalties and repercussions.* Clearly state the penalties for violations of the AUP. These need to be upheld, decisively and quickly, if a violation occurs.

If you want to participate in an ongoing discussion on the writing, implementing, and revising of acceptable use policies, join the K–12 AUP Listserv. Send an e-mail message to <k12-aup-request@merti.edu>. Leave the subject line blank and in the body of the message type <subscribe your first and last name>.

Sample Acceptable Use Policies can be found on numerous educational Web sites. Take a look at the following ones.

gopher://ericir.syr.edu/11/Guides

gopher://riceinfo.rice.edu:1179/00/More/Acceptable/fla

http://www.nmusd.k12.ca.us/Resources/Policies.html

http://riceinfo.rice.edu/armadillo/

A legal and educational analysis of K–12 Acceptable Use Policies and Guest/Employee and Student Account Agreements can be found at http://www.erehwon.com/k12aup/index.html. For a list of frequently asked questions about acceptable use policies, try the site complied by Classroom Connect at http://www.siec.k12.in.us/aup/aup-fag.txt. For suggestions on creating School Board Policies in regard to AUPs, try http://www.pacificrim.net/~mckenzie/fnomay95.html.

ICONnect
Connect to the Curriculum Connections/Reference section of the ICONnect Home Page for current updated reports and documents such as ALA Bill of Rights, ALA Resolutions on filtering software, AUPs, etc.

INTERNET TRAINER'S RESOURCES

As an Internet trainer you need to constantly upgrade your skills, keeping abreast of new developments. Following are a few online professional resources to help you develop and maintain technology skills.

Classroom Connect

> http://www.classroom.net/

> Includes online activities for K–12 classrooms as well as keypal addresses, lesson plans, recommended sites, and "Internet adventures."

From Now On: The Educational Technology Journal

> http://fromnowon.org

> Jamieson A. McKenzie publishes this free on-line journal focusing on technology and education.

MultiMedia Schools Magazine

> http://www.infotoday.com/MMSchools/index.html

> This practical journal helps educators use technology effectively in their classrooms and libraries.

Internet Trainer Listservs

There are two Internet listservs that support the Internet training, Web4Lib and NET-TRAIN.

Web4Lib

The Web4Lib listserv supports the discussion of issues relating to the creation and management of library-based World Wide Web servers and clients. Particularly appropriate issues for discussion include Web resource selection and information in relation to existing acquisition and collection development procedures; cataloging and data issues regarding Web information; In-house patron access to Web servers (e.g., Netscape on patron-accessible computers); training staff or users to use the Web or to create Web resources. Web4Lib is specifically aimed toward librarians and library staff involved in World Wide Web management, but anyone is welcome to join the discussion.

To subscribe, send the message "subscribe Web4Lib your name" to listserv@library.berkeley.edu. To contribute to the discussion, send your message to web4LIB@library.berkeley.edu.

NETTRAIN

NETTRAIN is intended to be a forum or clearinghouse for the exchange of information, advice, and resources on training others in the use of the Internet. It also provides a medium for wide-ranging discussion of practical, theoretical, and philosophical issues regarding training in the use of the Internet. (See Figure 8.10.)

Just found this new online guide to interacting online. . . .
http://node.on.ca/support/interact.html

I teach an email class, and will also be repeating my Internet chat and
conferencing class in two weeks, and would like to start spending more time in
both these classes talking about the interpersonal dimensions of online
interaction . . . guidance to newcomers to mailing lists, newsgroups, and chat
rooms. . . .

I'm not just talking about the basic rules . . . don't type in CAPS, read the group
for a few days before posting etc. etc. I'm also thinking about interpersonal
pointers that don't get too much attention, such as:

a)   Try not to take it personally if no one responds to your posts. People may
     be preoccupied or simply not have anything to say on the subject.
b)   If you really want a response, ask questions . . . Better yet, present
     information, then ask questions. Also mention other members by name
     and respond to specific points they make.
c)   If some criticize you, don't criticize back. . . . (etc., etc. For more on
     dealing with online conflict, see my Beyond Flaming article
     http://www.windweaver.com/email.htm)

Just wondering what other pointers other have for interpersonal issues that arise
in newsgroups, chatrooms and on mailing lists . . . including the interpersonal
issues that are initially internal ones (such as "I'm not sure that what I have to
say is intelligent enough so I'd better not post, because someone

Figure 8.10
NETTRAIN is one of the leading resources for librarians, computing professionals,
educators, consultants, and others engaged in the use of the Internet.

NETTRAIN is a listserv for "net trainers"—which does not necessarily mean "net experts." Anyone who is responsible for, or interested in, helping teach others to use the wealth of resources available through the Internet is welcome. "NETTRAINers" vary widely in skill levels. Some are network managers at large research universities; some are free-lance independent trainers. Others are simply those who have found themselves assigned the job of training others to use the Internet because they have shown the initiative to learn a little on their own. As always, we learn best by teaching others!

NETTRAIN is not for individual "help" questions. As a rule of thumb, NETTRAIN is not an appropriate forum for "how do I do so-and-so" questions, but rather for "how do I teach others to do so-and-so" procedures. NETTRAIN occasionally posts reviews of new books, videos, and other materials about the Internet.

To subscribe to NETTRAIN, send an e-mail message to: listserv@listserv.acsu. buffalo.edu. Leave the subject line blank. In the body of the message type "SUBSCRIBE NETTRAIN Firstname Lastname." You will receive instructions on how to proceed.

There are also several sites on the Web for Internet trainers. Following are a few of the more useful one.

Charm Net Learning

   http://www.charm.net/learning.html

   Books, tutorials, and hint sheets for Internet learning.

Internet Resources

> http://www.brandonu.ca/~ennsnr/Resources/Welcome.html
>
> A collection of resources that are useful to Internet trainers, such as Internet guides, resources lists, FAQs, and more.

Internet Training Resources

> http://www.public.iastate.edu/~kushkows/itrain/itrain.html
>
> A basic list of Web sites, primarily university based.

Library of Congress Internet Resource Guide

> http://lcweb.gov/global/internet/training.html
>
> An excellent collection of resources for trainers. (See Figure 8.11.)

WebHound Trainer Manual

> http://www.mcli.dist.maricopa.edu/webhound/guide.html
>
> This guide is written to familiarize anyone that might want to lead a WebHound workshop. A WebHound leader does not have to be a guru, but he or she should be very comfortable with using a web browser and explaining it to others.

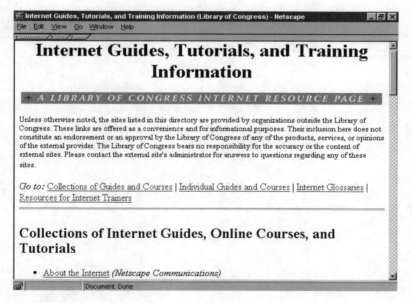

Figure 8.11

The Library of Congress Internet Resource Guide helps Internet trainers learn how to train others in use of the Internet.

Faculty, administrators, and parents need to understand the valuable and unique role library media specialists play in the integration of the Internet into the teaching and learning process. This will happen as more media specialists assume a leadership role in teaching the Internet. From the start, develop a network of other librarians and educators to share your ideas, support your work, and to continuously learn new aspects of the Internet.

NOTES

1. Based on ICONnect's online course *The School Library Media Specialist of the 21st Century* at http://www.ala.org/ICONN/onlineco.html.
2. Based on ICONnect's online course *The School Library Media Specialist of the 21st Century* at http://www.ala.org/ICONN/onlineco.html.

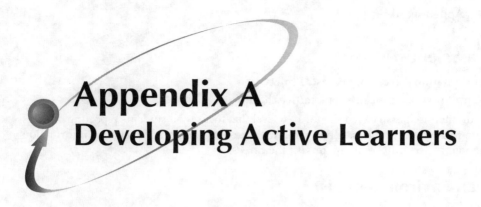

Appendix A
Developing Active Learners

Be a Historian

The New Deal Network

http://newdeal.feri.org

The New Deal Network encourages students to discover and document public works and private histories of that momentous time, as well as to publish their own stories on the New Deal Network.

American History Archive Project

http://www.ilt.columbia.edu/k12/history/aha.html

Middle and secondary level students locate digitized artifacts and historical commentary and are encouraged to make a contribution to ongoing scholarly examination of these resources through linked hypertext essays.

Civil War Publishing Project

http://www.rochester.k12.mn.us/john-marshall/overton/cwproj/main/civilwar.shtml

An ongoing project of students from Rochester, Minnesota, seeks contributions from students. They supply assignment directions and rubrics and your students submit original historical research papers to share with the world.

Be a Social Activist

Youth in Action Network

http://www.mightymedia.com/youth/

Focusing on the three components integral to participating in social action—Learn, Communicate and Take Action—this Web site is designed to help teachers, students, and concerned individuals from all over the world come together to engage in social action, primarily for environmental and human rights.

Be a Scientist

The International Trees and Forests Project

http://www.zip.com.au/~elanora/trees.html

An interdisciplinary Web site for K–6 level that focuses on students reporting on trees on their school grounds, telling about the seasonal changes, and including information about the creatures who live or visit their trees.

Be an Environmentalist

EnviroNet

http://earth.simmons.edu/

EnviroNet is a network of teachers, scientists, environmental educators and others who utilize telecommunications to enhance environmental science education. The purpose of the project is to enhance environmental science education at the middle and secondary levels in New England through the use of telecommunications. Activities include scientific monitoring programs, the sharing of ideas and data, electronic newsletters, and bulletin boards.

Be a Global Scientist

The Globe Program

http://globe.fsl.noaa.gov/fsl/welcome.html

GLOBE students make a core set of environmental observations at or near their schools and report their data via the Internet. Scientists use GLOBE data in their research and provide feedback to the students to enrich their science education.

Be a Dreamer

The North Star Project

http://www.fablevision.com/northstar/

A unique site that uses animation and wistful illustrations by artist Peter Reynolds to encourage students, teachers, and families to share their dreams for the future, create a constellation map, and nominate a famous "North Star."

Be an Artist

Children's Art Gallery

http://redfrog.norconnect.no/~cag/

A free exhibition space for students of any age. It has a flexible search engine to select artwork by student's age, subject or country.

Self*Expressing*Earth Online

http://www.onlineclass.com/SEE/SEEsub.html

This site, combines environmental education with expressive arts by inviting students to write poetry and stories, make comic books, act, draw, paint, and play music to re-awaken their personal and positive connections with the Earth.

Be a Zoo Intern

The San Diego Zoo InternQuest

http://edweb.sdsu.edu/edfirst/sandiegozoo/quest.html

Join ten California high school students as they recount their learning adventures as interns at the San Diego Zoo. Cast your Vital Vote on Conservation Habitat Plans and browse through the PhotoGallery.

Be a Mystery Writer, a Poet, or a Book Reviewer

CyberKids

http://www.cyberkids.com/

A futurist Web site for kids, this electronic publication provides opportunities for kids to share stories, art, or other creations; read a chapter a week from a new novel by a best-selling author; participate in real-time chat with other students; enter an International Writing and Art contest; and more.

KidPub

http://www.kidpub.org/kidpub/

More than 16,000 stories written by kids from all over the world. Set up a free page for your school to share their stories.

Midlink Magazine

http://longwood.cs.ucf.edu/~MidLink/

Midlink Magazine, an electronic magazine published quarterly for kids ages 10–15 in the middle grades invites you to "browse through our interactive space to enjoy art and writing that will link middle school kids all over the world. Every issue has a new and exciting theme. You can participate just by logging-in to these pages!"

The Book Nook

http://i-site.on.ca/booknook.html

The Book Nook allows students to submit and read peer book reviews organized by grade level and searchable by title, author, publisher, or keyword. Visit the Books Awaiting Your Review section, browse the "Lonely Books Club" to find books in need of reviews, or participate in an interactive conference area where students can enter forums or chat about current literature.

Diary Project

http://www.diaryproject.com/

An online journal writing experience in which students are invited to "share their thoughts, hopes, dreams, questions and ideas with other young people throughout the world via the Internet." Its inspiration evolved from the book *Zlata's Diary: A Child's Life in Sarajevo*, in which Zlata Filipovic shares her thoughts and feelings as a young girl growing up in Sarajevo.

Mind's Eye Exchange

http://www.win4ed.com/minds-eye/

A creative writing experience in which kids draw original monsters, write a description of the monsters, and share them with a cooperating school. Students from the cooperating school then try to redraw the original monster from the description.

The Looking Glass Gazette

http://www.cowboy.net/~mharper/LGG.html

The Looking Glass Gazette showcases stories, poems, artwork, book reviews, and other creative works by kids 13 years of age and younger.

Be a Journalist

KidChronicles

http://www.gsn.org/project/newsday/index.html

The Global SchoolNet believes that the youth perspective on life and learning and on local and world events is always a unique one. Fresh and spontaneous, it reveals insightful angles and dimensions that the adult eye sometimes misses. It's this perspective that Kid Chronicles features.

KidsNews

http://www.vsa.cape.com/~powens/Kidnews.html

KidNews is a free news and writing service for students and teachers around the world with over 2,000 young authors published. Anyone may use stories from the service for educational purposes only, and anyone may submit stories. They also invite comments about the news gathering, teaching, and computer-related issues in the Talk sections for students and teachers.

Be a Stock Market Investor

UISES

http://www.uises.com/sec/classrm.htm

UISES is a state-of-the-art investment simulation designed to give students practical experience in investment management and to foster a degree of familiarity with the technology that dominates the business world today.

Edustock

http://library.advanced.org/3088/

Created by high school students for the ThinkQuest competition, this interactive Web site teaches the essentials of the stock market, including a real-time stock market simulation.

Good News Bears

http://www.ncsa.uiuc.edu/edu/rse/RSEyellow/gnb.html

An interdisciplinary project specifically designed for middle school students and teachers, this project revolves around an interactive stock market competition between classmates using real-time stock market data from the New York Stock Exchange and NASDAQ.

There are also excellent telecollaborative projects that provide students with the opportunity to do authentic tasks. Listed here is a sample of telecollaborative projects. See chapter 5 for a background on this type of curriculum project and listing of Web sites to locate more projects.

Be a Geographer

North American Quilt: A Living Geography Project (telecollaborative project)

http://www.onlineclass.com/NAQ/NAQhome.html

Students will research weekly geography questions and contribute their findings to a "quilt of information" on the Web. Topics are based on the National Geographic Standards.

Be an Explorer

GlobaLearn

http://www.globalearn.org

GlobaLearn mounts live expeditions all over the world. Children, acting as the local hosts, provide an introduction to the community to investigate its history, traditions, industries, and physical resources. Using laptop computers and digital cameras and recorders, the explorers capture their discoveries daily and share them with kids via the Web.

Be an Archeologist

MayaQuest '97 (telecollaborative project)

http://mayaquest.classroom.com/

In the spring of 1995, '96, and '97, a team of explorers led by Dan Buettner bicycled to ruins in Mexico and Central America, met with on-site archaeologists and attempted to unlock one of the most perplexing mysteries of all time: the collapse of the ancient Maya civilization. But the team wasn't alone. Over 1 million kids, teachers and others from around the globe helped lead the expedition by way of the Internet.

Be a Scientist

Journey North

http://www.learner.org/jnorth/

From animal migration to tulip garden planting to interactive, comparative studies of the natural world, this project allows students to share collaborative data and receive daily reports. It presents challenging questions and on-line lesson plans for teachers.

Mythos: Zeus Speaks!

http://www.onlineclass.com/Mythos/MythosSub.html

In Mythos: Zeus Speaks! students follow the antics of the twelve major Greek gods and discover the foundations of ancient Greek culture as Mount Olympus goes cyber! Students read an on-going original story, The Incredible Adventure, participate in an e-mail interaction between students and the stories' characters to make ancient history (and imagination) come alive. Students learn both the fact and fiction of Greek culture from the gods themselves, as our e-mail moderator plays the parts.

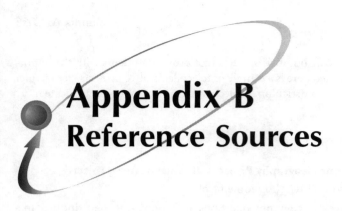

Appendix B
Reference Sources

(Based on CyberSites Column, by Linda Chapman and Phyllis DiBlanco, *Information Searcher,* Vol. 9, no.3.)

Arts, Literature and Writing

A+ Research & Writing for High School and College Students

http://ipl.org/teen/aplus/

Developed by the Internet Public Library, this site offers students guidance, support, resources, and links.

Academy of American Poets

http://www.poets.org/

The Academy of American Poets Web site provides a searchable database of the works of selected major poets.

All-Movie Guide

http://205.186.189.2/amg/movie_root.html

This searchable database of 131,000 films offers ratings, synopses, and links to other movies with the same themes or actors.

All-Music Guide

http://205.186.189.2/amg/music_root.html

This searchable database of 230,000 albums, plus song titles and artist biographies, includes all types of music except classical. Information about each hit includes ratings.

Complete Works of Shakespeare

http://the-tech.mit.edu/Shakespeare/

Contains all of Shakespeare's works, searchable by keyword. Includes related articles and recommended links.

English Server

http://eng.hss.cmu.edu/

From Carnegie Mellon, the English Server provides more than eighteen thousand electronic works. This site is excellent for students when they claim they have nothing to read, or when they would like to browse by topic.

Ethnologue: Languages of the World

http://www.sil.org/ethnologue/

The 13th edition of this electronic text contains links between 6,703 languages and the countries in which they are spoken.

On-Line Books Page

http://www.cs.cmu.edu/books.html

A treasure! Includes links to full-text books available on the Internet from several sites and includes foreign titles.

Quotations Home Page

http://www.lexmark.com/data/quote.html

Provides links to many quotation sites on the Internet, including Bartlett's 9th edition, published in 1901.

Roget's Thesaurus

http://humanities.uchicago.edu/forms_unrest/ROGET.html

The University of Chicago's ARTFL Project now includes Roget's Thesaurus (the 1911 edition, currently being updated). Although classified as experimental, this is a good reference tool for writers.

WebMuseum, Paris

http://sunsite.unc.edu:80/louvre/

Explore the WebMuseum's unique Famous Paintings collections where you have an alphabetical index to the works of the world's artists, a glossary, and a historical themes index. In addition, there are special exhibits.

Biography

Biography

http://www.biography.com/

This includes the searchable text of 15,000 entries from the *Cambridge Biographical Encyclopedia*.

CelebSite

http://www.celebsite.com/

This is an entertaining source of current information about celebrities. It's searchable and can be browsed by category.

Composer Biographies

http://www.cl.cam.ac.uk/users/mn200/music/composers.html

This site includes brief biographical sketches of some of the more well-known classical composers with selected links.

Literary Kicks

http://www.charm.net/~brooklyn/LitKicks.html

Includes biographical information of Beat Generation authors and poets and includes articles and samples of their work.

National Inventors Hall of Fame

http://www.invent.org/book/index.html

An electronic book; you may search for inventors and/or inventions.

The Nobel Prize Internet Archive

http://www.almaz.com/

Includes a searchable database of past Nobel Laureates, organized by prize and year. Entries include brief biographical information and varied links to related WWW sites.

Notable Citizens of the Planet Earth Biographical Dictionary

http://www.tiac.net/users/parallax/

This dictionary contains brief biographical statements on over 18,000 people from ancient times to the present day.

Business and Economics

Dow Jones Industrial Average Database

http://www.ipl.org/ref/stocks/

Provided by the Internet Public Library, this site provides quick and easy access to corporate and stock information for the companies in the DJIA.

1996 Fortune 500

http://pathfinder.com/fortune/fortune500/

Global 500:

http://pathfinder.com/fortune/1997/specials/

Courtesy of *Fortune* magazine, these two sites offer detailed information, including rankings, on the Fortune 500 and the Global 500 companies. Business and stock market news is also available.

Hoover's Online

http://www.hoovers.com/

Hoover's offers a searchable database of 10,000 major public, private, and international companies. Search the corporate directory by ticker symbol, name, industry, sales, or location.

Dictionaries and Encyclopedias

Encyberpedia Dictionary & Glossary

http://www.encyberpedia.com/glossary.htm

Although the graphics and advertisements on the opening page go on for too long, the links that follow take you to an incredible range of general and specific dictionaries and glossaries.

Foreign Language Dictionaries

http://www.june29.com//HLP/

Foreign language-English translating dictionaries are available at the Human Languages Page. Choose Languages and Literature.

Rhyming Dictionary

http://www.link.cs.cmu.edu/dougb/rhyme-doc.html

If you enter a word, the server will return a list of rhyming words.

Roget's Thesaurus of English Words and Phrases

http://www.thesaurus.com/

This is a searchable hypertext edition of Roget's Thesaurus, based on the text of the 1911 edition from Project Gutenberg.

Web of Online Dictionaries

http://www.bucknell.edu/~rbeard/diction.html

Includes links to 330 dictionaries in 100 languages.

WWWebster Dictionary

http://www.m-w.com/netdict.htm

An excellent hyperlinked dictionary and thesaurus based on the Merriam-Webster dictionary. The search engine supports wildcards and right-hand truncation.

Education

Educational Standards

http://putwest.boces.org/standards.html

The Putnam Valley School District site is the best place to go when you need information about national or state standards, documents, or curriculum frameworks in any subject area.

ERIC (Educational Resources Information Center)

http://ericir.syr.edu

To search for educational resources by keyword, follow the link to "search Eric database." Includes citations and abstracts for documents and journal articles published since 1989.

U.S. Dept of Education

http://www.ed.gov

A wealth of information is provided at this site, including programs, services, initiatives, grant guidelines, and links to affiliated sites and services.

History and Social Science

Background Notes on Countries

http://www.state.gov/www/background_notes/index.html

Provided by the U.S. Department of State, this site includes information on geographic entities and international organizations. (Note: To automatically receive via e-mail all newly released Background Notes, subscribe to the Background Notes listserv.)

Bureau of the Census (the Statistical Abstract of the United States, and more!)

http://www.census.gov

This rich site provides data about the people and economy of the United States and produces a wide variety of statistical products including :

The Statistical Abstract of the United States (http://www.census.gov/statab/www/)
The County and City Data Book (http://www.census.gov/statab/www/ccdb.html)
The TIGER digital map database (http://www.census.gov/geo/www/tiger/)
Trade Statistics (http://www.census.gov/indicator/ www/ustrade.html)
An up-to-date population clock (http://www.census.gov/main/ www/popclock.html)

Census Data, 1790–1860

http://icg.fas.harvard.edu/~hist1651/census/

From Harvard, this is a searchable database of historical, social, economic, and demographic data from the Decennial Census of the U.S., from 1790 to 1860.

City Net

http://www.city.net

This is a comprehensive guide to communities around the world. Includes a searchable interactive graphic world map and alphabetical index.

EuroDocs: Primary Historical Documents from Western Europe

http://library.byu.edu/~rdh/eurodocs/

This collection is composed of primary Western European documents (in translation, facsimile, or transcribed) from the Middle Ages into this century.

Geographic Names Information System

http://www-nmd.usgs.gov/www/gnis/gnisform.html

Provided by the U.S. Geological Survey, this is a searchable database for places in the U.S. by feature, state, or county name; feature type; population; or elevation range.

Government Documents at Yale

http://www.library.Yale.edu/govdocs/gdchome.html

Includes excellent links to a variety of government documents and other resources. An excellent site for social studies students.

Historic Documents of the United States

http://www.ukans.edu/carrie/docs/docs_us.html

Available through the University of Kansas, this site provides selected documents.

Historical Text Archive

http://www.msstate.edu/Archives/History/USA/usa.html

From the University of Mississippi, this site includes a link to Oklahoma's historical document collection as well as links to sites relating to specific topics in American history.

Mapquest

http://www.mapquest.com

This interactive Atlas allows you to find any place in the world. TripQuest provides city-to-city driving directions for the U.S. and parts of Canada and Mexico.

POTUS: Presidents of the United States

http://ipl.org/ref/POTUS/

Developed by the Internet Public Library, this is a comprehensive site on the American presidency and includes biographies, speeches and writings, election results, odd facts, and presidency highlights.

Stately Knowledge

http://ipl.org/youth/stateknow/

Courtesy of the Internet Public Library, this site will help you find the basic facts of any state in the Union, including Washington, D.C. Includes a searchable database, comparative charts, bibliographies, and more.

This Day in History

http://www.historychannel.com/historychannel/thisday/

From the History Channel, find out what happened on This Day in History. Includes historic events, celebrity birthdays, and chart toppers (music) for every day of the year.

Thomas

http://thomas.loc.gov

Provided by the Library of Congress, Thomas provides a searchable index to the Congressional Record. It also includes the full text of all bills submitted to the current and previous sessions of Congress.

U.S. Budget 1998

http://www.access.gpo.gov/su_docs/budget98/maindown.html

Provided by the Government Printing Office, the 1998 federal budget is available in spreadsheet and PDF formats.

U.S. House of Representatives

http://www.house.gov/

Includes information about legislative process, the current Congressional schedule, and listings of representatives and how they voted.

U.S. Laws and Law Library

http://www.house.gov/Laws.html

This site provides searchable access to the U.S. Code and Code of Federal Regulations as well as links to other law resources available on the Internet.

U.S. Supreme Court Decisions

http://supct.law.cornell.edu/supct/

The Cornell University Legal Information Institute offers Supreme Court opinions under the auspices of Project Hermes, the court's electronic-dissemination project. This searchable archive contains opinions of the court issued since May of 1990.

U.S. Gazetteer

http://www.census.gov/cgi-bin/gazetteer

You may look up places in the United States by name or zip code, and link to a detailed map and census data.

The World Factbook 1996

http://www.odci.gov/cia/publications/nsolo/wfb-all.htm

Chiefs of State and Cabinet Members of Foreign Governments

http://www.odci.gov/cia/publications/chiefs/chiefs-toc-view.html

The U.S. Central Intelligence Agency has recently released the latest in this annual series of country information reference books. Data is available for over 250 countries.

Washington D.C. Embassies

http://www.embassy.org

Information on all foreign embassies in Washington D.C.—address, phone number, e-mail address, and Web site URL. Listing of resources on Foreign Service, diplomacy, and espionage.

Flags of All Countries

http://www.wave.net/upg/immigration/flags.html

Color flags of all countries as well as maps and geographic, economic, and cultural information.

Zip Codes

http://www.usps.gov/ncsc/

The zip code directory site is provided by the U.S. Postal Service.

Math, Science and Health

BioTech Life Science Dictionary

http://biotech.chem.indiana.edu/search/dict-search.html

The Chemistry Department at the University of Indiana provides a searchable illustrated dictionary of over 3,700 terms relating to the life sciences and medicine.

Medline (Medicine Online)

http://www.healthgate.com/HealthGate/MEDLINE/search.shtml

Medline, the huge database of citations to medical, dental, nursing, veterinary, pharmacological, and related information, is available at no charge at Healthgate.

Unit Conversion Tables

http://eardc.swt.edu/cgi-bin/ucon/ucon.pl/

Courtesy of the EARDC Research Center at Southwest Texas State University, this site offers tables to convert any unit of measurement to any other unit.

Web Elements

http://www.shef.ac.uk/~chem/web-elements/

An interactive Periodic Table with links to key data and description of elements.

Fronske Health Center Health Education Site

http://www.nau.edu/~fronske/broch.html

Recommended for teenagers by the Internet Public Library, this site provides a collection of pamphlets on various health-related topics, from self-esteem to fitness to alcohol and drug use to AIDS.

Merck Manual of Diagnosis and Therapy

http://www.merck.com/!!rlyQv09xdrlyQv3AP6/pubs/mmanual/

This is a searchable version of the 16th edition of Merck Manual of Diagnosis and Therapy.

Periodic Table of the Elements

http://mwanal.lanl.gov/CST/imagemap/periodic/periodic.html

Courtesy of the Los Alamos National Laboratory, this site includes a keyword search of the table.

Scientists on the WWW

http://www.mwrn.com/feature/people.htm

This is a collection of searchable Internet sites that contain directory information about scientists working in the areas of biology, chemistry, virology, and microscopy.

Time-Life's Virtual Garden Electronic Encyclopedia

http://pathfinder.com/VG/

This is a searchable database that contains "almost 3,000 species selected for general use in North American horticultural practice." You can search by name or specific criteria such as lighting, type, and color.

News and Weather

University of Michigan Weather Underground

http://groundhog.sprl.umich.edu/

Current weather information for cities in the U.S. and around the world.

USA Today

http://www.usa.com

Contains current news, sports, arts, editorials, etc, from the newspaper.

The New York Times

http://www.nyt.com

National and international news.

Boston Globe/Associated Press

http://www.boston.com/globe/

Current news.

Colleges and Careers

100Hot/College

http://www3.web21.com/college/

Includes the top 100 colleges' Web sites ranked by number of hits, with links to each school.

College View

http://collegeview.com

Profiles of over 3,500 colleges and universities, electronic applications, career planning tools, and virtual tours of over 200 colleges.

Peterson Directory

http://www.petersons.com

Valuable resources on K–12 schools, including distance learning.

Occupational Outlook Handbook, 1996–1997

http://stats.bls.gov/ocohome.htm

Published by the Bureau of Labor Statistics, the complete text of the OOH is available online and searchable by keyword.

Miscellaneous

Associations on the Net

http://ipl.org/ref/AON/

From the Internet Public Library, this is a searchable annotated guide to more than 550 home pages of prominent organizations and associations.

FAQ Finder

http://ps.superb.net/FAQ/

This is a comprehensive guide to more than 1800 FAQ (Frequently Asked Questions) files available on the Internet, arranged by category.

The Kelly Blue Book

http://www.kbb.com/

Guaranteed to interest high school students, this searchable database is an excellent source of information about the value of new and used cars.

The National Address Server

http://www.cedar.buffalo.edu/adserv.html

Given a valid U.S. postal address, this server rewrites the address in the proper format along with the ZIP+4 code. You can retrieve a Postscript or a GIF file of the address for printing, with a barcode! You can also view a street map of the address, from two different Internet map sites (MapBlast and MapQuest).

Phone Books and Directories

http://thorplus.lib.purdue.edu/reference/phone.html

Courtesy of Purdue University Libraries, this site provides links to phone books and directories from around the world.

Appendix C
Parent Resources on the Internet

50+ Great Sites for Kids and Parents

http://www.ssdesign.com/parentspage/greatsites/50.html

An American Library Association site that includes top sites for preschool and elementary school children and their parents to explore together.

Berit's Best Sites for Children

http://db.cochran.com/db_HTML:theopage.db

This site offers a large selection of rated Web sites including sections on Just for Fun, Holidays, and Creatures Great and Small.

Child Safety on the Information Highway

http://www.4j.lane.edu/safety/

The National Center for Missing and Exploited Children's guide to Internet safety for children.

Expect the Best from a Girl. That's What You'll Get.

http://www.academic.org

Produced by Mt. Holyoke College, this site provides information for parents to help their daughters succeed.

Internet Resources on Disabilities

http://busboy.sped.ukans.edu/disabilities/

Maintained by the University of Kansas, this site provides excellent links to disabilities resources.

The Children's Partnership

http://www.childrenspartnership.org

Offers, for free, the full text of its useful guide, The Parents' Guide to the Information Superhighway: Rules and Tools for Families Online, prepared with the National PTA and the National Urban League.

The National Parent Information Network

http://npin.org

Cosponsored by the ERIC Clearinghouses on Elementary and Early Childhood Education and Urban Education, it includes extensive articles on parenting, listservs, and links to more than 100 sites on education, health and safety, family issues and interests, and parenting and development of children from infancy to adolescence.

National PTA

http://www.pta.org

Learn about PTA education programs and participate in a discussion group, chat room, or bulletin board. The site also includes links to sites of many organizations concerned with children.

The Family Education Network

http://www.familyeducation.com/

Offers hundreds of brief articles on parenting, links to local sites, and discussion boards that connect parents with online experts.

The Partnership for Family Involvement in Education

http://www.ed.gov/PFIE/

Sponsored by the U.S. Department of Education, highlights school-community-business partnerships and includes a calendar of events.

Department of Education

http://www.ed.gov

Parents will find information about the President's education initiatives, college financial aid, and parenting publications, along with links to other useful education sites.

The National Coalition for Parental Involvement in Education

http://www.ncpie.org

Provides a catalog of resources available from all its member organizations.

Parent Soup

http://www.parentsoup.com

Includes an archive of answers to questions asked of pediatricians and child development experts and advice about helping your children succeed in school.

The Parents at Home Site

http://advicom.net/~jsm/moms/

Especially for at-home parents, offers e-mail pen pals, booklists, and links to children's sites.

Steve Savitzky's Interesting Places for Parents

http://www.crc.ricoh.com/people/steve/parents.html

A comprehensive site for parents to explore children's issues on the Internet, software links, educational sites, and many other resources.

Zero to Three

http://www.zerotothree.org

Provided by the National Center for Infants, Toddlers, and Families, an organization devoted to child development, this site offers research and information to parents on the social, physical, and cognitive development of infants and young children.

The White House

http://www.whitehouse.gov/WH/New/Ratings/

Describes a strategy to involve government, industry, parent, and teachers in putting together a rating system so parents can define material they consider offensive and protect their children effectively.

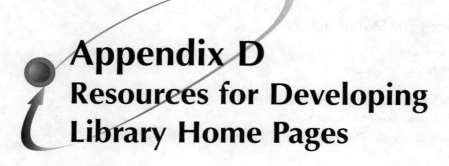

Appendix D
Resources for Developing Library Home Pages

Understanding HTML

A Beginner's Guide to HTML

http://www.ncsa.uiuc.edu/General/Internet/WWW/HTML Primer.html

HTML Crash Course for Educators

http://edweb.gsn.org/htmlintro.html

Includes interactive components.

Writing HTML

http://www.mcli.dist.maricopa.edu/tut/

Kevin Werback's BareBones Guide to HTML

http://werback.com/barebones/

Lists HTML tags for quick reference.

Wade's HTML Tutorial

http://webproduction.miningco.com

Learn about the most frequently used features of HTML in JumpStart.

An Example Page That Makes Sense

http://www.dcn.davis.ca.us/~csandvig/ip/example.html.

Top Fifteen Mistakes

http://www2.dgsys.com/~hollyb/top15.html

Practical advice on what not to do in designing home pages.

Beyond the Son of Filamentality

http://www.kn.pacbell.com/wired/beyond/

This Web site provides 30 online tutorials designed to customize HTML pages.

Learning HTML by Example

http://jeffco.k12.co.us/high/awest/learnhtml/00conten.htm

Resources for Webmasters

Cyberbee Web site
http://www.cyberbee.com

Web Tools: Essential Resources for Web Weavers
http://schmidel.com/webtools.htm
Contains help with HTML, design and links to software for Webmasters.

Webmasters Resource Page
http://www.perkin.net/pekin108/webmasters/resources.html
A site devoted to school Webmasters.

Web Pages That Suck
http://www.webpagesthatsuck.html

Resources for Creating an HTML Document
http://www.tiac.net/users/eberne/jantools.htm
A good resource for developing school library web pages.

Webspinner's Workshop
http://dcn.davis.ca.us/~lacarrol/webspin.html
Contains over 13 categories of resources for the Webmaster including tips, tools and graphics.

TableMaker
http://www.bagism.com/tablemaker/
A form-based Web site to help create forms for home pages.

Carlos' Forms Tutorial
http://robot0.ge.uiuc.edu/~carlosp/cs317/cft.html
Learn to create Web Fill-in-Forms which allow the user to submit information to the web server.

Color Maker
http://www.bagism.com/colormaker/
Choose a color for your web page.

Texture Land
http://www.meat.com/textures/
Includes more than 250 textured backgrounds.

Clip Art Resources

Library Media and PR
> http://www.ssdesign.com/librarypr/toolbox.html
> Contains great free library clipart, including ALA graphics.

Olson's Library Clip Art
> http://www.chrisolsom.com/ALAsymbols.html
> Includes major library symbols.

Library Graphics
> http://www.geocities.com/Athens/Acropolis/2161/
> A collection of book and computer images.

HTML Goodies
> http://www.cs.bgsu.edu/~jburns/gifs.html

Icon Browser
> http://www.cli.di.unipi.it/iconbrowser/
> A huge selection of images to browse or search.

Icon Bazaar
> http://www.iconbazaar.com/cons.html
> Thousands of clip art images by category

GIF Animation on the Web
> http://members.aol.com/royalef/gifanim.htm
> Contains information, tutorials, and samples.

Welcome to Fefe's Transparency Apparatus
> http://www.inf.fu-berlin.de/~leitner/trans/english.html
> Makes a GIF image transparent.

Jelane's Free Web Graphics
> http://www.erinet.com/jelane/families/
> Great collection of graphic "families."

Image Paradise
> http://www.desktoppublishing.com/cliplist.html
> Lots of links to free clipart.

The Web Developers Virtual Library of Icons
> http://WWW.Stars.com/Icons/
> All the icons are on one page.

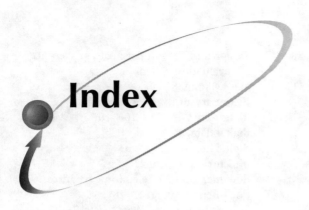

Index

Pam Berger is a school library media specialist at Byram Hills High School, Armonk, N.Y. and the publisher and editor of Information Searcher, a newsletter for integrating technology into the curriculum. She is coauthor of *CD-ROM in Schools: A Directory and Practical Handbook for Media Specialists* and has written numerous articles in library and education journals. Berger has presented at conferences in over 30 states in addition to Canada, Singapore, Thailand and Switzerland. Her Web site "Information Searcher Online" features CyberTours, interactive Web tours designed for educators to learn curriculum integration strategies. She is chair of ICONnect, the American Association of School Librarians' national technology initiative.

DISCARD